You Can Always Come Home

"Growing up in the South in a good but deeply flawed family, there's always that certain warmth with coming home…that feeling for me that I can relax. That I am always loved at home. In reading the heartwarming stories of *You Can Always Come Home*, I found myself reminiscing on so many beautiful moments of coming home. Laura's artful storytelling will stir some of your fondest memories of life, those memories that make life worth living. Plus, I have a sense that I'll treasure the memories as they are being created more, too."

Mike Zeller,
Business Coach, Speaker, Mentor, *Author of The Genius Within*

"Laura, you and I and everyone have two things in common: we all have a past and we all have a future. Laura's winsome storytelling will encourage you as you follow the breadcrumbs of your past toward a hopeful, redemptive tomorrow. I'm a sucker for Southern culture, and if you are too, you'll find yourself in her stories. It's a must-read!"

Rebecca George,
Author of *Do the Thing: Gospel-Centered Goals & Gumption and Grace for the Go-Getter Girl* & Host of the *Radical Radiance* Podcast

"Laura Jean Bell's book *You Can Always Come Home* has a magical way of making you feel like you're sitting on her porch, savoring sweet tea together. It's a heartwarming memoir that beautifully highlights the importance of family, storytelling, delicious food, and faith. I found it hard to put down, as it wrapped me in the cozy embrace of Southern charm as I read."

Ashley Petrone,
Author of *Designed to Last,* @arrowsandbow on Instagram, Owner of Joie Inn and The Fox Mercantile

"When I think of people that embody the spirit of Jesus, Laura Jean Bell tops the list. Laura is someone you want to sit on a front porch with, nursing a cup of coffee or tea while you are filled up with down-to-earth wisdom and hope. *You Can Always Come Home* is just that, with all the best Southern anecdotes from an author who gets what it's like to live in a world that feels inhospitable at times. Laura knows how much to guide others home to the truth while inviting you to her table of hope."

Chrissy Powers,
MA LMFT, Embodiment/Trauma Therapy Coach,
Creator of the Embodied Woman Group Coaching

"We all want to belong, and my friend Laura shows us how, no matter where we may find ourselves. Vulnerable, honest, and wise, Laura uses her beautiful gift of storytelling to stir our own hearts to remember—to look back over the shoulder of our lives and to give thanks for the people and experiences that have shaped us. She encourages us to take time to taste the memory or to make the phone call, which may prove to be a step towards exactly what we are in need of. Laura reminds us ultimately our belonging is in Christ, in whom we will always find arms outstretched, offering us hope and, in the truest sense, Home."

Katie Kizziah,
Wife, Mother of Seven, Writer at An-Open-Journal.com

You Can Always Come Home

FOLLOWING THE BREADCRUMBS OF YOUR PAST
TO FIND THE HOPE OF YOUR TOMORROW

LAURA JEAN BELL

NEW YORK

LONDON • NASHVILLE • MELBOURNE • VANCOUVER

You Can Always Come Home

Following the Breadcrumbs of Your Past to Find the Hope of Your Tomorrow

Published in New York, New York, by Morgan James Publishing. Morgan James is a trademark of Morgan James, LLC. www.MorganJamesPublishing.com

Proudly distributed by Publishers Group West®

Morgan James BOGO™

A **FREE** ebook edition is available for you or a friend with the purchase of this print book.

CLEARLY SIGN YOUR NAME ABOVE

Instructions to claim your free ebook edition:
1. Visit MorganJamesBOGO.com
2. Sign your name CLEARLY in the space above
3. Complete the form and submit a photo of this entire page
4. You or your friend can download the ebook to your preferred device

ISBN 9781636982649 paperback
ISBN 9781636982656 ebook
Library of Congress Control Number: 2023944217

Cover Design by:
Nalin Crocker

Interior Design by:
Christopher Kirk
www.GFSstudio.com

Morgan James PUBLISHING **Builds** **with... Habitat for Humanity®** Peninsula and Greater Williamsburg

Morgan James is a proud partner of Habitat for Humanity Peninsula and Greater Williamsburg. Partners in building since 2006.

Get involved today! Visit: www.morgan-james-publishing.com/giving-back

To my husband, Cody:

They say two dreamers can't marry. And to that I say,
"Says who?" Cody, you never once doubted that I could write
and publish a book. I'm still jaw dropped I snagged you—
my sounding board, my best friend, and my biggest champion.
Thank you for the sacrifices you have made and the unwaver-
ing belief that I am, without a shadow of a doubt, worth it.
We are worth it. This is for you.

To Emmy Lou, Oaks, and Lottie:

You are my living, breathing testimonies that God was faithful
then and He is faithful now. Each of you is a miracle I didn't
know was possible. Thank you for being the faces that keep me
going when life gets hard. I love you. I'm proud of you.
"You're my favorite part of every day."

Table of Contents

Foreword

*I*don't write forewords. Ever since I began writing books shortly after the close of the Civil War, it's sort of been my policy to never write forewords.

The first reason is because forewords are dumb. And I am not good at writing them. Namely, because I can't ever figure out how to spell foreword correctly. Foreword is not the same as forward. Sometimes even autocorrect can't figure out the difference.

FACT: In the process of writing this, autocorrect has changed foreword to forward six times.

So if you learn nothing else from this foreword, remember this: Foreword means an introduction to a book written by someone who is (hopefully) not the author. In this case, *moi.* Whereas forward means moving toward something.

Don't say I never taught you anything.

So, anyway, the second and most important reason I don't write forewords is because nobody ever reads them. And even on the rare occasions when people actually do, nobody cares about them. You know it's true. Don't lie.

Take me. I am a big reader. And yet I cannot remember ever picking up a book and saying to myself, "Wow, what an outstanding foreword." Usually, I open the book and promptly skim past the foreword, and begin looking for the pictures.

Well, if that's you, scanning through this current foreword, the good news is: we're almost done. But the even gooder news is that you're in for a treat with this book.

This book first came to me from my friend Laura, who sent me her manuscript—real friends do this to each other—when I had no time to read it. Which is not her fault. I keep myself too busy. I don't even have enough time to read important highway signs while driving.

But here's the thing. I did read her book. I stayed up for about an hour each night to fit in a few chapters here. A few chapters there. And I loved it. Which is no surprise; Laura is a terrific wordsmith. And I believe you will love it, too.

Now, in the tradition of literary forewords, this is the part where I am supposed to tell you something anticipatory about the book, such as: "This book made me laugh, made me cry, made me want to be a better American, and helped me pay off my mortgage in less than three months."

But I'm not going to do that. Because the truth is, even though this book actually did make me do some of those things, you don't need me to sell this book to you. Because you're already holding this book. Which means you're supposed to be holding it. Because things happen for a reason.

So quit reading this dumb foreword and start reading the actual book. Because I think these words will make you feel something. I don't want to summarize Laura's book here, but the following pages will feel a lot like taking a stiff shot of grace. The same kind of grace that propels you ever onward.

Toward home. Upward. Skyward. Heavenward. In other words: forward.

Sean Dietrich
Storyteller, Musician, Author of *Will The Circle Be Unbroken* and *You Are My Sunshine*

Introduction

She stood quietly fixing her dress and hair, then reached down to pick up her newborn baby. The two of them walked slowly and quietly to the front of the sanctuary.

The baby was new—the kind of new where they sleep so sound and peaceful, especially when tucked in the arms of their mama. And Mama was eighteen and scared and bold and, well, everything you would need to be in a Southern sanctuary to bring forward your words of wisdom to those a year behind you. You see, just a year earlier, she was a graduating senior. There was a lot ahead for her.

And then, within a few months, she was pregnant. It was clear that this circumstance was not planned. I don't really know any more details than that. But neither did the rest of the church. We just knew she was officially a new mother, and it was a little bit scary for her.

Our preacher called her forward to speak in front of the congregation to share advice that she would tell herself if she could go back a year in time. As she got to the microphone, our pastor stood there proudly, waiting to hear her words of wisdom for the graduating class. (Senior Sunday is a big deal, a tradition we have held on to as a church for decades where we celebrate seniors graduating by sharing a quick slide show, giving them each a new Bible, and throwing a fancy after-church potluck.)

But this year was different; our preacher had rallied together the seniors from the previous year to share their wisdom, their "I wish I knew then what I know now." Each recent graduate went forward, one by one, sharing their thoughts on college and what to do and what to care about, all of it a little immature, yet kind. We watched each current senior gobble up the words. Then came her turn. She hadn't gone to college yet and she had the look of a tired new mama on her face.

She stood at the mic and looked at our pastor, who looked back at her with confidence and reassurance. She looked at the seniors and her eyes filled with tears. She looked around at the entire church body for a few moments as she silently wept and looked down at her baby.

In a soft, emotion-filled voice, she mustered out, "No matter where you go, what you do, or how long you're gone, you can always come home."

She waved her arm out over the whole audience of church members. "And no matter how far you go, home will always be a part of you."

We all caught it. We all felt it. The young, the old, the middle-aged, and the college kids, we caught it. She had experienced it. All of us at some point had experienced it.

Don't tell me I am the only person who has crumbled the moment you hear your mama's voice on the other end of the phone after a hard day. It's why we can be walking down the street and smell honeysuckle starting to bloom and be transported in time to the days when life was as simple as finding one of those bad boys on the church playground and trying to eat every single one of them before your friends found it too. It's why when we have a bad day, we can shut the door to our car and blast an old song by ZZ Top and think about the things our dads told us as kids that made the world make sense.

It's why any time you smell eggs on a cast iron, you think about your grandmother and how much you wish you could have one more conversation with her, even if it is about nothing. It's why three hours after you get dropped off at college you call your mom in a frenzy about not understanding what taking sixteen hours means and you cry your eyes out the moment she answers the phone.

We all caught it that day. We all felt it. Because we all, no matter what has happened in our lives, have home wrapped up in a warm blanket in our souls. And we know that the world can turn upside down and we need home; we need to find our belonging, our healing, our identity, and our hope all over again.

I've worried a lot about the people in my life who don't have the memories of honeysuckle or ZZ Top, or who cry at the sound of their mama's voice because their parents were cruel and their home was covered in trash. Maybe they, too, felt like trash, like their identity was made up of the very people that had brought them into this unforgiving world.

But that's not really home, is it? Smell memory and taste memory are deeply personal and confined to the reality of your rearing.

The reality is that home is *Him.* The one true, kind, loving, personal, intimate, merciful Father who redeems it all. The One who made you so vastly perfect that returning to home in your heart is all you need to go running back to Him. After all, He made you just like Himself. Your birth certificate may tie you to a family of dysfunction, but worthiness is your birthright from the Giver of good gifts. Life is a gift, and the Giver is good, amen?

So we return. We return to the sounds and smells, the sights and the moments. The ones that remind us to return to who we were made to be. The return is scary, the way returning back to the father was hard for the prodigal son, and we feel undeserving, unable, incapable, too broken…completely burnt out on trying to be the good kid, whatever that might be.

We return. And when we do, we find that all along, the stories of our lives draw us back to Him. And we find moments that remind us He really was there all along, even in the dark moments where we were certain that He wasn't. Where we wondered who the heck we were. Where we wondered if anyone wanted us around. Where we wondered if we could heal from the indescribable heartache. Where we wondered if we could truly, one day, laugh at the days to come.

That girl, in a single breath, summed up the whole glory and beauty of the goodness of God. We don't know who we would be in a circumstance until that circumstance happens. She walked to the front and showed a body of believers the reality of what it looks like to carry the weight of the world on your shoulders at eighteen years old and yet, still, be carried. Carried by friends and family and her church. She showed us what it looked like to run home and say, "How do I do this? I don't know what to do." She stood before all of us and reminded us that it wasn't about being perfect or doing the thing that would get you the best career or make you a millionaire before the age of thirty. She reminded us that returning home is the best thing you can ever do, because it's where you find the person you were meant to be all along.

A staple show in our house growing up was *Everybody Loves Raymond.* Right before the world turned on its head and decided to become offended at just about everything, there was the humor of Ray Romano, the spot-on feature of a family living in Queens and navigating life with small kids and intrusive in-laws. Although over-dramatized, the accuracy of the conflicts and the hurts, the misunderstandings and the nuances of marriage and parenting, are so spot on.

My husband and I were watching the episode about Amy and Robert's wedding. Even if you aren't familiar with the show, we all know that every wedding episode has some speech that is either the magical moment or the moment of complete catastrophe. In this particular episode, the speech is hilarious. The jokes and the discomfort can be felt through the screen as Ray gives an ode to his brother and new sister-in-law. With his unplanned speech he is able to string together words that make the ending a stunner—after all, he is a writer.

After sharing a slew of jokes, Ray shares about the value of editing. There are good moments and bad ones, the days where you want a do-over. If you are married, you don't remember every moment of that day, but you do remember what you want to remember. You remember the good stuff. I personally remember my photographer pushing me to do a first look with my husband. I didn't want to but ended up agreeing. As I walked toward him, I started bawling and telling him to turn around because I couldn't take the anxiety. I can still see his face turning toward me and every fear melting.

This. This is where we find the good stuff. The God stuff. Where we take the memories of smells and tastes and people and moments of joy and of pain and we find Him again. Wrapped up in each moment. It's where we remember why we do any of it.

I want you to remember the good stuff, the God stuff. The moments where He helped. Lock in the memories that remind you who you are and where you come from. As time goes on and the pace of life becomes faster and the demand for more becomes overwhelming, just remember the good stuff. The life before things became too fast.

Let's open the sock drawer and dig around for the memories we stuffed in there long ago. Let's sift through the moments that broke us and find the healing we have been hungry for. Let's remember the people who showed up when nobody else did and reminded you that you belonged. I hope you'll see the moments that secure the confident piece of you, and that you'll hold on to that for dear life. I hope you learn to laugh again at what the future holds. Because what comes next is going to be your best story.

It's waiting for you in these pages.

Life is waiting for you in these chapters.

Let's live it all over again, together.

This is just the beginning. Praise the Lord, this is just the beginning.

If you made it this far, I hope you know that's what this book is about: home. It's about the people and the places that make up home. The food we can taste in our sleep, the moments that were regular until our memory of it made it extraordinary. It's about the men and women who showed up and taught us something worth being taught and didn't know they were changing our life. It's about faith and family and remembering as to never forget it. It's about laughter and stories that help us make honey for our souls. It's about learning that hope is there for us, even when all seems lost.

More importantly, it's about remembering that no matter what happens, the good, the bad and the ugliest of ugly, you can find your way back to the person you were made to be. It isn't over just because it feels like it is; if you're breathing, He is working. Underneath all the layers of baggage and messy you can find yourself again here; you can find home.

This book you are reading is one that I have wanted to write for years. Nine years to be exact. Right after I walked off that stage carrying the diploma that I feared I wouldn't get because school wasn't exactly where I thrived, I have dreamed of this.

This may surprise my readers, but I walk around the world a very outgoing, extroverted, bubbly person, who for most of my life thought that my personality was all I had—kindness, love, the ability to see others' needs without them ever telling me. And then, I wanted to write a book. But money. But someone else needed me. But one person didn't like my writing. But I may not be good enough. But nobody will read it. But...imposter. I couldn't bring a single word to paper so I resorted to blogs because they were safe, and the internet wasn't yet skewed with a million other streams of social networks. I took the assistant jobs I hated, and I worked crazy hours for little pay and I settled for nonstop because I didn't believe for a moment that I was worth more than that.

I finally realized the only person holding me back was, well, me. Reliving the moments that jarred me or healed broken pieces of me—that's what this is all for. It's why I had to write anything in the first place. I had to write it because I had to say yes to the worth and the stories God put smack dab into my heart. I had to relive to heal, to stand in belonging, to thrive in my identity, and hope recklessly for my future. To be more bold, more calm, more boundary-ed, more of who God made me to be. I had to find home again, with the Lord, within myself.

This book is my journey. How I learned in all the nooks and crannies of my life, all the sporadic memories tucked in the crevices, that what remains—in my life, in all our lives—

is home.

In one single moment, on one little Sunday in May in one little church, in one town in the deep south of Alabama, in one tiny little sentence, one girl with a newborn baby reminded me there is one thing in this life that will never leave you.

Home.

You can always come home.

Part 1
BELONGING

CHAPTER 1

Stop Calling and Just Show Up

few months before we found out we would be moving to our little farm community of Arab[1], Alabama, I was driving down County Road 1807, the road that leads to every cousin, great aunt, uncle, and extended somebody. All this because one man decided to leave an inheritance to his children's children, then went and had nine kids to leave it all to. So here we are, the descendants, still hanging around on one long county road.

I made it to the three-way stop that corners a farm store, a field of trees, and Miss Maxene's house. Nobody reading this will know Miss Maxene, but if you did, I know you'd love her as much as I do. Probably more. But on this particular day, as I glanced in the direction of her house to make sure nobody was coming, I felt a tug in my spirit: *You need to talk to her.* I

---

1   Arab is pronounced "Ay-rab," with the accent on the first syllable.

shrugged it off as nothing short of a coincidence or a plague of guilt. I hadn't really laid eyes on this saint of a woman in probably five or ten years.

Maxene is a matriarch in the community, a kind woman who befriended my grandmother in high school and the two talked every week until the day my grandmother left this earth. In fact, just moments after my grandmother passed and the coroner had taken her body, Maxene pulled into the drive carrying her famous angel food cake for a visit with her friend.

I ignored the nudge in my spirit and made my way back to Montgomery, where I went about my daily life. Every day I would feel the nudge, *You need to talk to her.* For nearly two weeks I would think of Maxene and shrug off the tap in my spirit. Finally, one day, I felt the nudge during my toddler's naptime and thought, *I'll write her a letter.* So, I did.

I wrote a letter that had nothing to say other than, "You were on my mind. I hope you are well. Maybe we can talk on the phone sometime," followed by my cell phone number, nothing more.

Roughly a month after sending that note, I received a phone call.

"Laura?" the woman said on the other line.

"Yes, ma'am?" I replied.

"It's Maxene. I got your letter."

"Oh wonderful. How are you?"

"Doing all right, I suppose."

"Good!" There was a long, awkward silence.

"Well, it was good to hear from you. I'll talk to you soon," she said and we ended the phone call. I thought the nudge must've just been in my head.

Months passed, I visited the farm and back multiple times and never said another word to Maxene.

By the end of July 2020, every plan my husband Cody and I had made for the year imploded on us. The school we planned to attend "went solely online," leaving us locked into a year lease in a town we no longer had a need to live in. Our apartment was packed and ready to move just forty-eight hours from the moment we received that email. We realized our best option was to leave our home and community and all we had built and move to the small community that had only ever been a getaway for a few family reunions and time with my grandparents.

This wasn't home. This was the place I was thrown. I felt tossed in and abandoned. My grandparents had gone to Heaven. Every person within a mile was working full time. I had no school or sports events to use to connect with other families. Churches were all closed and "online only" due to "the virus." I was now uprooted from my hometown and circle of friends and transplanted to a cabin in the woods with a toddler and a few cows. I didn't work full time, I couldn't connect to a church home, and the isolation nearly broke me in a way I don't think I have ever experienced before.

It was nearly surgical.

An undoing of sorts.

For an extrovert like me, this transition that Cody and I both knew the Lord had prompted us to take slowly began to feel like cruel and unusual punishment.

I just needed connection and friendship, someone to call or go on a walk with. *Coffee date, anyone?* But even those events felt grueling. Being new has a way of shattering you and exhausting you to the point of no return. *How many times will I have to explain how I ended up here?* I wasn't even sure I could tell the story without bursting into tears and attempting to pack my bags and go back to what felt normal—what felt *safe.*

One day, in a fit of self-pity, I remembered the phone call months before from Maxene. So, I called her. On a whim born out of desperation for someone to talk to.

And she answered.

And told me to come over.

I loaded up toys and cookies and coffee and my toddler Emmy Lou and showed up on my best behavior with hands full of treats. Maxene barely touched the treats and drank zero coffee. She smiled and doted on my daughter. She laughed and listened to me ramble on to fill awkward silences.

Maxene isn't exactly a chatterbox, but it made room for the copious number of words I needed to release. Before I could come up with the next conversation piece, Maxene looked me in the eyes and said, "So why did you want to visit with me?"

I sat there, not sure how to respond, when a thought ran across my mind that I spilled out before thinking about what I was saying. "You were my grandmother's best friend. I don't know you like I should. I figured it was time."

Maxene's eyes filled with salty tears as she managed to say just a few words, "I miss her every day."

I cried with her.

But not just because I missed my grandmother, because I do. But my eyes were opened to the "why" behind the prompting I had felt months earlier. The Lord knew that the two of us would be lonely. Lonely in a way that couldn't be described.

Maxene was in her home sun up to sun down, and her best friend—whom she had called or seen three days a week—was gone. And so was her husband.

I had been uprooted from my hometown and my plans for "the next step" were crushed. All of my closest friends now lived hours from me and were continuing life without me around. Nobody cared that I was here and understandably so; they had lives to live.

But Maxene and I were now comrades. Two women who missed their friends and found themselves in a state of loneliness that, some days, felt suffocating.

The weeks continued in this little community of ours and the loneliness did not lift. But I saw Maxene every week. Some days, it was the only thing I had to look forward to. A friend who was actually there and didn't mind my company. I didn't have to explain my people to her; she knew them all. She even knew the ones I never got to meet. She knew what was hard and what was easy and she made me feel less and less like the outsider that I was.

I finally realized that I needed Maxene MUCH more than she needed me. Or maybe even wanted me for that matter. I would call and try to bring treats and goodies and we would visit together for about an hour. Some days we would just laugh and stare at Emmy Lou while Maxene would let her tear her house apart in the most toddler way possible.

There were days I would sit and talk and spill my guts and bawl my eyes out about life being hard and challenging. Maxene always listened. She still does.

The best part: I knew anything I said would stay right there between us.

One Wednesday night, when we first moved, Cody and I got into the car and drove to every church on Main Street looking for a Wednesday night class to join. Every church door was locked. I went to Maxene's house the next day and felt crushed by all the avenues I was trying and feeling like I was failing or running into brick wall.

Of course, Maxene's church was still open. A congregation of seventeen people still met each week and the ladies met on Wednesday nights. So, she invited me to her Wednesday Bible study that was ACTUALLY meeting and most weeks I would go home with dishrags she knitted for me.

The Bible study: *Life in the Wilderness.*

It felt divine. It probably was.

One day, as I was walking off her front porch from a weekly visit, Maxene said to me, "Don't call, hun, just come. I am always here."

So, I stopped calling ahead.

I just went when I wanted to.

That's when it hit me: we may not have a million things in common. She grew up in a totally different world and generation than me. She hasn't moved from home; I was uprooted from mine. But Miss Maxene taught me the true art of friendship. It's not about perfect cookies or treats or experiences.

Maxene taught me how to stop callin' and overthinkin' and just to show up. That's all anybody ever needs in this world. Push past the awkward conversations and niceties and learn that, when your life turns upside down or you become the old lady in the community who is still living when everyone else around you is dying, you realize…we don't need perfect, we just stinkin' need each other.

I don't know how much Maxene needed me. But I needed her. I continue to need her.

Life got better; life got easier. Churches opened and things slowly returned to how they used to be. I made friends my age and met women with kids my kids' age. I joined the Mothers Club in town and started doing service projects. I learned who was who in town and became a regular at the coffee shop.

A few months ago, at a Mothers Club meeting, one of the women in the group told me she had read a story I wrote about Maxene on my blog. She asked about her and told me how much she loved my story. I started talking and as I spoke, I realized all that had changed since I first started going to see Maxene. One of my siblings had moved in next door. I had started a new business venture of my own. We had planted our feet in a new church and friendships had begun to blossom through preschool, church, and familiarizing myself more and more with the town.

As I spoke, I started to cry. I kept apologizing because I couldn't finish my thoughts without weeping in front of this new friend.

Maxene was my first friend here. The one who wrapped me up and told me that I was going to be okay. She didn't ask anything of me; she just let me be. She didn't make me feel like the new person and I didn't have to explain to her a hundred times over who I was or who my parents were. I didn't have to prepare anything or do my makeup or tell someone where I was from all over again. I just got to show up. With a crazy toddler and empty hands and a heart that wanted a friendship.

Now we come to her house, and she pulls out pictures of herself and my grandmother in their prime, going out on double dates with their beaus. She tells me stories that remind me we have overcomplicated our purpose in this life and in turn it has truly hurt our ability to LOVE the place we are in when we are in it. She so lovingly gives us small gifts of coloring books and crayons and time spent on the front porch for Emmy Lou to watch "big tuckssss dive by."

It's not rocket science.

It's just showing up.

It's being a friend when it's messy and when it's easy. It's letting someone into your life without all the accessories to try and prove yourself as someone worth being with. I tried to offer it all and she made sure I knew that wasn't what made me worth being around. It was me being me. It was me being someone who remembered her and her best friend.

It's amazing when we zoom out after the storm seems to have calmed and we take a good hard look at the way it all fell together. The way the Lord pushed us together in comradery and helped knit together a friendship of two lonely women who needed the façade to fall off. We needed to laugh at something together and find hope for what might be coming next. My kid needed to be around someone who let her be unabashedly herself and Maxene needed someone to gift her dish rags to.

I know the Holy Spirit prompted that letter in April 2020. He was preparing me to remember that no matter where I go, I can belong. Just because someone has lived somewhere their whole life doesn't mean they don't need a new friend. And just because I am new somewhere doesn't mean I don't belong.

He taught me that showing up and making the first move is what He did. When He befriended the orphans and the widows and the tax collectors and let the little children come to Him, He did the awkward thing that became the most important thing of all: giving us all a place to belong.

We can leave what we know, and we can stay and never move. But belonging, it's what we are made for. It's the showing up that's the true cure for the loneliness we may feel. And when we do the thing that feels awkward, often it ends up being the greatest gift we could ever ask for.

CHAPTER 2

Get Used to It

We have a myth on our hands: we believe we are in control of our own lives. Don't get me wrong; we are in control in that we are able to decide for ourselves and mess up and try again and thrive. But then things happen that remind us of the astronomical number of things outside our control, and it scares us to death. That was me in 2020. Wasn't it all of us, though? Waking up and thinking, *What happened? How did I get here? Now what?*

There was the pandemic. I had just moved from a big city to a town of only a thousand people. I had left my community and everything familiar. At every turn I was lost as to how to even operate. *Where do I go to the doctor? What should we do for fun? How long does it take to get to town? Is there even a gym here? For the love of God, I miss Target.*

I was fresh and nervous and sad and so unearthed out of my routine. Nothing in the town made sense to me no matter how hard I tried. I wanted home. Space. Community. I wanted life to make sense again and not feel so polarizing. I wanted it not to smell like cow poop or chickens, or a combination of the two. But this was the world I was in and the giant I had to face.

What do we do in times like this? In a "now what" season? I pulled out my magnifying glass. I put everything into the lens of what I wished the situation could be, not what it was. This approach was safe. I wanted to exist within my own comforts and for others around me to simply just understand, to get me. This approach was safe, but it didn't work.

How I was living was prohibiting anyone from doing what I desired most. I believed I had to build a life that only showed my best self, never letting the negative, unfortunate pieces of me emerge. I was living in the same challenging world everyone else was living in, but I believed mine was somehow more challenging. Only I had something to prove. Everyone else clearly had it together.

Four p.m. was the hardest time, the late afternoon before Cody would get home. Emmy Lou and I would be home together, bored and cooped up in the house or out in the yard. So, one day I decided to take her to the park as a means of escaping whatever depressive state was headed my way. We played and ran around the playground and tried our best to tune out the noise of loneliness in my mind. Afterwards, I decided to stop by a local coffee shop to grab a treat for us.

Walking into the coffee shop, I saw a group of women from a church we had visited a time or two. They were having a small-group gathering and invited Emmy Lou and me to join. Within minutes, I met a girl who lived just five minutes away from me or, as she put it, "a four-wheeler ride away." Soon, I was planning a coffee date for her and another friend to come over to my house.

A week later, I was getting coffee made and everything prepped for these new friends to come and sit on the porch for a visit. I walked outside to make sure the chairs were clear of leaves and bird poop and was welcomed by an odor that, simply put, smelled like death. I was so upset. *WHY do I have to live in the country with this horrid smell? Why do my cousins next door have to take all the cow manure, kill it, then spread it and kill it again? Can you kill cow manure?* If cow manure can be killed, this was what it would smell like.

I picked up my phone. "Friendly warning: It smells like something died. Either on one of our pastures or my cousins'. I am investigating but it smells awful, and I won't be offended if you don't want to come."

Within the same minute of sending the text I received a reply: "Used to it." Followed by, "Yeah, it will just smell like home. I live between two chicken houses. No smell can ruin this night."

Despite the quick responses, I still felt anxious. But when they arrived they didn't even bat an eye at the smell of the yard. They drooled over the porch, the cozy feeling, the coffee being so good, the friendship we had formed. We connected the dots that my dad's first-grade girlfriend was one of their great aunts. We laughed and connected and I shared all the quirks that made no sense to me as they nodded and said, "Yep, that's north Alabama for ya!"

I tried to keep myself from being rejected and not seen as a desperately lonely girl living in a cabin in the woods. But the truth was, I was the desperate lonely girl living in a cabin in the woods. And plain and simple, the things that scared me left no mark on them. They barreled their way through like the fine wine my soul needed in that season. It wasn't really about the smell of the coffee, or if the chairs had bird poop on them; it was about having connection after a year of being told by the news, friends, and even some family that we couldn't. It was about making friendships that last after grasping for just a taste of community again. It was about settling into what normal would be in this small town and finding out quickly that I would soon be creating friendships that would encourage me.

And, that one day, without blinking, I would think of it and say, "Used to it."

When did we get to a point where we feel like we have to explain ourselves, or like we have to explain every single thing that might make someone question us, our home, our lives, or even something completely out of our control? I had to get used to the concept of real life and let go of the illusion that we have control over what other people think. Is that what we want? Let's be real: is that what any of us want? To feel so controlled by the opinions and thoughts of others that we start drowning in the anxiety of their thoughts before someone even has a chance to think them?

When I was twenty-five, a lady at church looked at me dead in the eyes and said, "What someone thinks about you ain't none of your business; stop making it your job to know." I wish I listened to her sooner. There's been countless hours of my life where I have bowed to opinions and run further and further into the arms of affirmation, only to find out that validation has an expiration date. Once it goes bad, we have to start hunting for it all over again. I can't live like that; none of us can. It's exhausting to believe that we can. Our seasons are our seasons. And Lord have mercy, there is grace for that. There is even mercy and grace for the seasons that are busting at the seams with life and abundance and community and joy.

My new friends, their kindness and their "country-ness," nourished me in a way that I never knew I was lacking. I didn't have anything to prove and neither did they. I wanted to prove myself worthy of a new friend because I wanted one so bad. But, I didn't have to. I didn't have to lay everything out in hostess perfection. They made themselves at home. Even started opening drawers looking for spoons as they searched my fridge to find creamer.

Some weddings today may still do this, but do you remember receiving lines? Where you stand in one place and everyone comes by and you receive them, thank them for coming, and basically just let them love and dote on you for however long they so choose? I think that's what we are supposed to do. Just receive it. The kindness that comes easy. The people that don't expect you to become anything perfect, they just want to know you.

These girls showed up to my porch—two single girls with testimonies that would light your soul on fire. I had never met people so willing to just say it like it is, just to make the Lord shine bigger than He could even shine. They were single at the time and because of this night of coffee on a porch with the smell of death swirling around us, I got to watch one of them get married to a man she prayed she would meet. In that season, she had no clue who he was.

Here's the thing on belonging somewhere: some days it takes massive effort and some days you get to stand in the receiving line. You'll find hope and healing. You'll look back and think about the memories that flood you with laughter and joy. Get used to the fact that things in life break down, like our need to show the perfect side of us, and then they heal up. When they do heal, they're stronger for it.

Most of the time, it is about being willing to have compassion for yourself, asking the Lord to show you a new way to meet Him and love Him because the old ways aren't working. It's about standing alone in an old cabin in the woods and abandoning the identities that you were certain you couldn't live without. And one day you'll wake up and remember the night where you got to be the bride in the receiving line, standing and shaking hands with people who just want you. Not what you could give, do, be, act, portray… nope, just you. All because you believed for a single second that you really do belong.

CHAPTER 3

Atlas Dinners

ody and I spent two years trying to find a church. Hunting and searching and joining small groups and walking into churches and making small talk with all the people. I knew quickly how much I hated being new, but I don't think I took into account how painful it would be. But we finally found the church that fit, the one where we felt a part of it and people knew our names and our child's name and invited themselves to our house to help with the chicken harvest. It was unlike anywhere I had been since leaving home.

I spent twenty-eight years of my life being the consistent expert in my hometown, especially my home church. So, when we were church hunting, I would pray and ask the Lord for help and guidance every time. A cry of repentance would rise up in me for every single new person I remembered seeing roaming the halls of my home church for twenty-eight years and I never once stopped and introduced myself. They, too, were likely nervous and emotional and so completely raw and I was rooted, well-adjusted, and the expert in the place they were visiting. But, "I didn't feel like introducing myself."

This process began a review in my mind that pushed and urged me to stop and think and reflect on my life "before the move." What did I do to make friends? Were they just built into the hometown, or did I actually have a skillset that I completely lost when we moved away?

The two things I found in the cobwebbed, dust-covered trunk of memories buried in the back of my brain were lines my parents repeated to me a thousand times over: "If you ask someone about themselves, you won't have to come up with much to say"—advice I had never really put into practice—and, "When in doubt, invite someone over for supper."

Supper.

The final meal of the evening. Let's remember this: Southerners have always said this correctly. Yankees call it dinner, but the Lord himself called it the "Last Supper," so who REALLY is right on this one? I digress.

I worked hard at this.

At our new church, I was determined to invite any person I could convince to come over for pot roast or even Domino's pizza and I would ask them a million questions about themselves. It would be my journey to meeting people and convincing them to make the trek out to our land. Because I needed community, I needed people.

One night after church, still fresh with this congregation, I was cleaning up the children's area. I had been staying in class with Emmy Lou to help her adjust to the new surroundings and surprisingly got to know lots of people this way. The pastor's wife, Katie, worked in the class with me that night and we really connected. I felt the Lord come right in front of me and say, "Ask her to supper." I might have looked overly enthused, but I blurted out, "I wanna have you over for supper."

Her grace filled the room as she said. "Let me talk to my husband. We would love that." Mind you, this family had five children, with a sixth on the way, and I realized I was asking her to haul her whole crew over and out to the sticks for a meal. It could be a lot.

In a weird mood, I texted her and decided on a whim that I would offer two options, "You come to us OR I will cook and bring it to you. Whatever is easiest." As a recovering people pleaser, I can spot another PP (my nickname for those of us who still need some rehab) from a mile away and I could smell her inability to say what she wanted. I shot out an option I had never offered before.

Make dinner and bring it to her house? What in the world was I thinking? Honestly, I wasn't.

She lit up at the idea of us bringing the supper to them.

We arrived and her five kiddos walked out like ducklings to help offload the food out of my car. She had drinks and cups and plates and her husband had even gone to the church for extra ice. I made a pot of spaghetti, sourdough bread, and salad. We got to know their kiddos and scarfed down the food just in time for the ice cream truck to roll in. All the kiddos ran outside for ice cream and the dads joined them like more of the crew.

Once everyone had eaten dessert, their kids grabbed ours and took them off to play and we actually got to sit and enjoy adult company. (All my mamas nod and say amen.)

They were kind and polite and doing what pastors do… pastoring without knowing. It's like they just instinctively know how to pour into everyone around them at all times. They asked us a million questions. That's when I remembered that they were once missionaries in Africa. Our pastor, David, mentions it in sermons from time to time and even takes groups back there. I felt my brain reeling and remembered watching my parents host suppers with international students at their house. My Dad would pull out his atlas and have each student flip through it to show where they lived.

Another trick of the Plunkett family trade. Ask them about them. So I did.

"I wanna know about Africa. Tell me where you lived."

We talked about where they'd lived and what they'd done, how it was getting overseas with children and HAVING children overseas. The cultural differences. The life where electrical power was short-lived and unpredictable. They told us stories of seeing Jesus in different places and realizing that being a missionary was so much less about changing others than it was about really changing yourself.

They made a pot of coffee and pulled out clear, glass coffee cups that had the atlas on them in white. When black coffee fills up, the atlas pops.

They pulled them out specifically for us.

We made our way to comfy couches and I continued to ask questions.

Katie shared about moving back the States. How life was so different. David was working a new job and working nights. They made their way to be with her family and she was so looking forward to telling everyone about Africa and people being excited that they were back. But nobody, not a soul, seemed to notice and nobody asked. How isolating.

I imagined how lonesome it might be for people to hug you and see you but to be unseen. She shared that on their last day with family for Christmas one of her family members said, "Tell me about Africa," and she nearly crumbled. How emotional it felt that someone saw her and saw that there was a life behind her that she deeply missed and grieved. Saw how much she wanted to talk about it and share and tell. I nearly cried listening to her.

Katie knew what it felt like. She knew from working with me in the children's ministry on Wednesday nights that I was new. She asked the questions and connected and knew how to do that because she had once walked around a world of people who saw her but didn't see her. She once was the new girl who was trying to speak a language she had never spoken and mother children amongst a new culture, a season she grew to love and cherish so deeply. Then, after years of doing big things and hard things, she had to go be new again, in places where nobody cared about Africa or the things that mattered to her.

Let's be real: we can't convince the world to care about all our needs or the big parts of our hearts. But we can grow and heal and shift and change and become the people who help others belong. It's not too late to turn around and see the new mom walking into preschool and invite her for coffee and ask her a hundred questions about herself. It isn't too late to stop in the hallway and introduce yourself to a new family that just walked through the doors. There's still time to belong but, more importantly, I am learning there is still so much time to help someone else feel like they belong too.

If you think you're too old to do the whole belonging thing, you're not. When I was halfway through my freshman year of college, I transferred to a school back home. I was new in my own hometown, which felt weird. Every other week when I was in school, I would eat lunch with a lady from church who was ninety years old. She would have me over for lunch and the two of us took care of one another for a while—a memory I will carry forever. Mrs. June is in Heaven now, but she's in my heart forever. Why? Because it is never too late to make that difference. There's still time to grow into something you never thought you could grow into.

Man, I tell you.

There's just something about suppers in the South, a tradition I don't think I ever want to let go of. I hope we all remember to just open up the door and let people in. But the most important family tradition I learned, which may be the best trick of all the trades, is asking someone else to tell you about them. Pulling out an atlas and letting people point to what matters to them. Because that right there is where the magic happens, when kinship grows, when loyalty flourishes, and when people finally realize that they aren't alone after all.

CHAPTER 4

Poppyseed Chicken Casserole

*M*y family has always been the family of inviters. Along with the atlas dinners for international students from the university where both my parents worked, they are always inviting over new people visiting the church. My mom picks from a few of her staple meals that have always been a crowd favorite: pot roast, poppyseed chicken casserole, or some meat on the grill for my Dad to smoke while mom makes bread and salad, all with a tub of Bluebell in the freezer for dessert. They are the masters of hospitality, and they do it so frequently it has become their norm.

Hospitality is engraved in the identity of a true Southerner. We don't realize how inviting we really are, because the inquiring of life in a grocery store line is simply second nature. But we know that showing up with a dish in hand when there is a birth or a death is the most important act we can offer. Food. We know no other way to bring about the love and admiration of a new baby or to comfort a mourning soul like taking the load of cooking off of the person in that new season and bringing a pan of fried chicken and something with a sour cream base. (We like our saturated fats.)

When I had Emmy Lou, I was still living in my hometown. The meal train set up for me by the church was filled up with weeks of homemade meals delivered to my door—so many meals that my mother actually called the church office and set up a cutoff date to make sure we didn't overwhelm the system.

When I moved away, everything in the hospitality realm felt weird. This was no longer my territory. I was no longer the master direction giver. I was no longer asked to host events. I was the new girl who didn't know where to get my license renewed and could not for the life of her find where the Walmart in town put their Q-Tips.

The month we moved to Arab, a girl I met at a Bible study invited me to come to an Usborne Books party at her house. She welcomed Emmy Lou and me to come and eat snacks and learn about these books from a local girl in town, the wife of a youth minister at a church in the city who sold books as a side hustle. I went to the party reluctantly because I was so very homesick and insecure, but I knew showing up was better than panicking out. So, I went. I knew there would be chatter and communion among women who had lived in their small town together for a long time and there was a large chance my inclusion in their chatter wouldn't be welcomed. That was okay with me, I decided. I would go anyway.

My thoughts and expectations rang true within the first ten minutes. My nerves were on high and I decided to just sit on the floor with Emmy Lou, who was twenty months old at the time, and play with her as a distraction.

"Are you new to town?" a voice behind me asked.

Finally, someone asking me a question.

"Yes I am; we moved here just a few weeks ago," I said.

"Where from?"

"Montgomery."

"Oh, Montgomery! I had a ton of friends in college that were from Montgomery."

Excited to maybe know a mutual soul, I dug deeper and found out she was friends with three of my closest friends from back home.

She sat with me and made conversation. She took the load off of me to be the initiator and allowed me to be the interviewee. We exchanged phone numbers and mentioned the idea of getting together sometime soon.

Then I got miraculously pregnant with our second baby. Cody and I were thrilled and overwhelmed. It was quite the season of transition and life was beyond all consuming to begin with. There was the new church we had started attending and getting involved. We were serving on the hospitality committee and me in kids' ministry on Wednesday nights. We attended every service and had even started learning a few names and faces. But, mostly, people didn't know us, we still had no close friends, and life was still exceptionally lonely.

My pregnancy got harder and harder with each passing day and my life felt as slow and awkward as my body. I wanted so desperately to find my place and kept feeling like I was walking around in two left shoes.

To my surprise, just two weeks before I had my son, the gal from the book party sent me a text. "Hi friend, I know we never ended up getting together. But I would love to have you over for coffee. Let me know a good day."

Reluctant and still homesick, I made the effort to go and try. Being new gets exhausting. You show up and have to tell the same story one hundred times over. People don't know who your dad is or where you went to high school, nor do they care. They want to know about the present you. Even if the present version of you could crumble into tears at any given moment. Even if present you resents living in that town and that place and wants a way out of it. I was terrified of her meeting the present me because present me was so tired and so pregnant and so very sad.

We had coffee and we chatted and shared funny moments and mutual friends. Her hospitality was the breath of fresh air I had hunted for months and wasn't finding, no matter how deep I dove into our church or farm community. I wanted close, intimate relationships like the ones back home. The ones that took me five plus years to build. I was weary and looking and she somehow remembered me and brought me in for a cup of coffee on the hottest day in June. Claire was new and kind and inviting.

I had my second baby; we named him Oaks. It was the height of the Delta variant of Covid and people were still wary of visiting or showing up for one another. The silence of our door on the country roads was haunting for me in that season. My mom came and my mother-in-law, but the meal train was never set up. The church we attended at the time never called or offered a meal or lent a hand. Sadly, they didn't even know we had had a baby. What once was so full and energetic and exciting with our firstborn was so silent and isolating with our second, enough to make my heart sink at the lack of people who seemed to care outside of our own family. We were blessed in other ways, don't misread, but lack of community was the one thing I feared, and in that season I was facing the very thing I had hoped so much to avoid.

There's a weird sickness that comes with the fear of rejection, which is maybe greater than the fear of lack. The two are pretty much the perfect dysfunctional relationship we dread. We don't want to admit that we fear it or that it even plagues us. But it does. We want to pretend that we don't care to be a part of the mom group at the preschool or that it doesn't bother us when people talk about their friend gatherings in front of you. We want to seem brave in the face of the dangerous perils of lack. They have friend gatherings; I don't. They chose them and not me. It sounds so kindergarten but somewhere inside each of us is that little person longing to be remembered by someone. It's lonely in the adult world. We have to find friends, stay in touch, wrangle babies, and learn how to run a home all while just needing your people to show up and say I love you and how can I help.

One day, sitting on our porch and rocking my new baby who simply would not sleep unless held, I heard the crackle of gravel on my driveway. Sitting with my parents and husband and newborn baby we all looked at one another and wondered who could be coming down the half-a-mile-long driveway. The unknown SUV pulled up, parked, and as the door opened, there was Claire, smiling and waving while unloading salad, rolls, and a casserole all wrapped up in an aluminum to-go pan. I could weep now just considering the thoughtfulness of someone who really had only spent one afternoon hanging out with me. She did what her raising had taught her: take food to people with a new baby. Show up and show the love.

Outside of my family, Claire was the only person who came. She showed up and touched my newborn's toes and met my parents and I awkwardly explained how we knew one another from one book party and a coffee date a year later. She slipped away and continued to check in every few weeks to make sure I was hanging in there okay. She had two kids of her own and knew the struggle of the one-kid-to-two transition in the home. All along, I felt like she was the person who stood in the gap between lack and rejection and said, "I see you. You don't have to work for it."

Claire and her husband would end up planting a church in Huntsville and leaving our town to chase after more souls for the Kingdom. Life would move on. It's how seasons go. They never come to stay. Thankfully, people like Claire let us know that the hell we are walking through will eventually end. The wounds will scab over and eventually heal so much that you can barely see the scars.

The church we were attending ended up shutting down and we finally found a church family where it was easier to plug into Sunday school classes and fellowship suppers. We made more friendships and community than we had in the two years since moving to the town.

Fast forward to the time of this writing. A few weeks ago Cody had to have ACL surgery. I was sitting in the hospital, waiting for him to get out of surgery, when I received a text from my sister with a link to a meal website. I opened it up to see two weeks' worth of meals scheduled for us starting the day after we would get home from the hospital. It wasn't a new baby or death but a debilitating surgery and the people we knew were rallying and doing what they knew to do. Feed. It's that southern DNA again and, honestly, I don't know how people in the Yankee regions survive without it in their bloodstream.

I sat with the Lord for a moment. I cried. I thanked Him. Humbled by the souls who saw fit to choose to sacrifice their time and money and energy to bring us food and care for our family. It was redemptive and a loud reminder that life moves on, and God will make good from moments that broke you.

That season of Covid loneliness and a newborn gave me a clearer vision of what it looks like to see the new person not as a stranger, but as someone who just needs someone to talk to and ask them about their life. They need someone to see them and fill a need that they didn't have to ask to have filled. In the waiting room of a hospital, the Lord redeemed that hurt memory. He reminded me that though the suffering in that season felt so loud, there was one person who showed up. Claire reminded me that even though I had left behind every ounce of belonging in one city and had come to a new one, I could belong here too.

I learned in that dreadful season and moment of my life to be a Claire to the new girl in town. That I should probably be the type of friend I hope someone else would be for me. And maybe, I should learn how to make my mother's poppyseed chicken casserole.

Southern Poppy Seed Chicken Recipe

WHAT YOU'LL NEED:

- Rotisserie chicken
- Medium yellow onion
- Cream of chicken soup (if you are gluten intolerant, grab the gluten-free version of this soup!)
- Sour cream
- Cream cheese
- Poppy seeds (optional)
- Salt and pepper
- Butter
- Ritz crackers (or a similar gluten-free buttery cracker)

HOW TO PREPARE:

1. Shred the rotisserie chicken and finely dice your medium onion.
2. Mix it all up: in a large mixing bowl, mix together cream of chicken soup, sour cream, softened cream cheese, poppy seeds, salt, and pepper. Add the shredded chicken and onion. Then give it a good mix again.
3. Spoon mixture into bottom of casserole dish. Use a rubber spatula to evenly smooth chicken mixture in the bottom of the dish. Put crackers in a zip-top bag and crush with your hands, then top the chicken mixture with them. Drizzle with melted butter and sprinkle on

extra poppy seeds. Bake at 350 degrees until bubbly and golden brown.

Serve with rolls and southern green beans!

*This recipe is delicious served with rice—totally optional.

PART 2
IDENTITY

CHAPTER 5

Chocolate Pie

*M*y mom had jumped into the deep end of a phase. Do you know what I mean by a "phase"? Phases are the center point for people who lean toward the spectrum of ADHD. They hyper fixate on something for a period of time before it becomes something they aren't willing to hyper fixate on any longer. Maybe the fixation was just boring all along and they finally realize it or maybe the fixation made their pants too tight.

On this occasion, my mother was still knee deep in her newest phase: Chocolate Pie. Not just any chocolate pie, but the one her mother was famous for making. My mother is known for her sweet tea, her Thanksgiving dressing, and making the simplest of meals slap. The woman can cook. But there is one thing that she simply cannot do well: bake.

There is an art to both cooking and baking: some people have both and some people only have one. I pray for those who simply have none. My mama can cook, and she will tear a kitchen to bits when she does. The woman spends 95 percent of her holidays on the phone with friends and siblings telling them how to make something as simple as cornbread. But, when the woman bakes, she burns. She forgets ingredients. She sets the oven too high or too low or she sets a timer and never hears it go off. She simply cannot do it.

I'm not the only one to admit this; she herself will look you clear in the face and tell you the trouble she has with baking. She once took a loaf of rosemary garlic bread that I had just finished and said, "I think we need to toast it a bit longer." Instead of disagreeing with my mother, I obliged and let her make the call. Next thing I know, she is pulling out my bread that took me four hours to make, burnt to a crisp.

She poured me a glass of wine and apologized.

I still haven't forgiven her.

But this phase, this phase of her life, was becoming something that might change the trajectory of her bad days of baking. This hyper fixation on "Mama Jean's Chocolate Pie" might be the turning point to make her a both/and. She might just become both a cook AND a baker.

It started when she went to a party where someone made my grandmother's (her mother) pie. Just a few short years after my grandmother passed away, her best friend decided to gather up her recipes and create a cookbook in her honor. It was such a treat and brought in all the best recipes you can imagine from my grandmother's kitchen, her chocolate pie being one of them.

My grandmother, Jean, was known for her pies. She made one nearly every Saturday. A Saturday afternoon treat with a cup of coffee. I hope one day to slow my life down enough to whip up fun pie recipes every Saturday as a treat. Her chocolate pie was what she was known for: golden crust, chocolate center that had cooled long enough to be just the right density, and meringue perfectly browned on the top. Always lovely and, when cut into, it looked like it should be on the cover of a magazine.

My mom, when hearing that the host had used her mother's recipe, leaned in. She listened, she decided, she fixated, and she went to work.

I will perfect my mother's chocolate pie, rang in her head the remainder of the year. From the middle of summer until Christmas Day, she worked on this pie and making it just like her mama did. I watched on the sidelines as she burned the crust, forgot ingredients, produced runny chocolate insides, and whipped meringue that never set.

But she never quit. The grit she carried to make this pie was strong. Cody and I willingly ate her mess-ups, enjoyed eating runny chocolate (forget perfect density, that chocolate center was divine). She eventually got there. Christmas Day, she made a pie and the crust was golden and the chocolate was firm and the meringue was perfectly browned on top. We celebrated with an afternoon coffee and a slice of pie. What a treat.

I asked her why she cared so much, and her answers would waiver between, "It's just something fun to practice," and, "I have no idea." Finally, in a small conversation over pie and coffee, with the kitchen covered in flour and sugar and melted butter, my mama said, "If I don't learn this, it may become a recipe none of us share with anyone else."

That's when I decided that we don't have to have the perfect answers for our hyper fixations. (Yes, I have them too.) Sometimes, we need to hyper fixate to taste something again. Maybe for some reason our soul is hungry for the time that has passed and desperately wants to feel it again. Even if it only lasts as long as you sip a cup of coffee. Pie is not important. Being both/and is simply not the point. The point is that my grandmother passed away sixteen years ago and some days it feels like yesterday when the grief billows up out of nowhere. Some days, it feels like she's been gone longer than she lived.

There's something you should know about Southerners: we love moving forward and playing the long game. We are the agricultural center of the nation, for heaven's sake. We know the long game and leaning into working through the hardships. But a Southerner knows the secret to the joy of life because we believe in the remembering of it. Not just thinking. But telling.

The stories we share match the food we eat. It's the reason we keep the rolling pin that doesn't roll because it once rolled out the world's finest biscuits. We are the guardians of the memory. The storytellers who want the stories to stir our hearts, to change our minds, and to make way for future plans. We want our food to spark the memory of the best Labor Day weekend or our favorite Saturday with our mama when she lived next door and our kids were young and life felt heavy and hard and confusing and overwhelming—but mama had pie. And coffee. And she was there.

Maybe my mama wanted to be a both/and. Maybe she wanted a to become both magical cook and chocolate pie baker. But more than anything, I think my mama wanted to be with her mama again. Maybe to her it looked like stirring up another batch of chocolate and sugar and forgetting the dash of salt and licking her wounds and chocolate-covered spoon to try again the next day. Because some days, we need to taste the past again. We need to remember who we are and know we can get back there. Even if it takes us months to get there, we need to sit down and have a slice of pie and a cup of coffee with Mama again.

Life is fussy and fuzzy. We can't control the story as it all unfolds, no matter how much we want to. We lose people, some leave us on purpose, and some get taken. We need to remember the people who made us feel like nothing else mattered because it helps us remember who we are.

I think my mom's deep-end pie-making phase is reminiscent of what the Lord wants from us. He wants to pick up our pieces, the identity of worthiness and safety and security that sometimes feels shaky, and help us remember that, no matter how many chocolate pies it takes, He is the one living within us, drawing us to the better versions of ourselves. There will be hard days and mundane days. God is in both. There will be goodness in today and grief in tomorrow. God is in both. Pain and loss are going to be a part of all of this for us. It isn't a punishment for living; it's just a consequence of location and the whole Adam, Eve, and serpent thing. Life will bend us and break us, but we will get put back together.

My mom lost her mom, her best friend, her confidante, and the one she called about everything. She makes pies to remember her and taste a part of herself again. With every bend and break, we get stronger and braver and older and, thankfully, more free. We will get there eventually, but God is in every burnt crust and licked spoon along the way.

Mama Jean's Fudge Pie

WHAT YOU'LL NEED:

- 1 cup sugar
- 3 tbsp cocoa
- 2 heaping tbsp flour
- Pinch of salt
- 1 cup milk
- 3 large egg yolks
- 1/4 cup butter
- 1 tsp vanilla
- 1 eight- or nine-inch baked pie crust

HOW TO PREPARE:

1. Mix dry ingredients together.
2. Mix milk and egg yolks and add to dry ingredients. Cook in a heavy saucepan over medium heat until thick, stirring constantly. Add butter, let melt.
3. Remove from heat and add vanilla. Pour the cooked chocolate filling into baked pie crust. Top with meringue and bake at 350 degrees for 10 minutes.

MERINGUE:

3 large egg whites
3–4 tbsp sugar

Beat white until foamy and then start gradually adding sugar. Beat until stiff peaks form but whites aren't dry.

CHAPTER 6

The People Who Made Me

*G*rowing up, I always thought my family was odd. My mom wasn't the cool mom and my dad wore jeans on the beach. I was their third child and the youngest grandchild, so the care to be cool was whittled down to bare bones by the time I started school. I was safe and loved and cared for, listened to and laughed with and given ample attention, blah blah blah. My life was good but our family's level of cool was minimal, at best.

The older I get, though, the more I realize that the parents who let their kids drive out of town at sixteen unsupervised, the moms who let their daughters wear strapless dresses to Sunday school, and the Dads who didn't use phrases like, "I didn't fall off the turnip truck yesterday, darlin'"—people who had grand-parents who didn't show up to their dance recitals or sit on the porch peeling peaches and telling stories, or parents who didn't make you write interview questions to ask your great-grand-mothers and grandparents, filming them so you could watch it when you were older and hear their voices again—were actually less cool than my parents and grandparents.

We wanted to press down our "uncool" parents and tell them they were embarrassing us all those years, but in reality, they were just making us as cool as they are. Giving us the space to think and dream but be protected from the things we were simply too small to carry. I think I forget that the people who spoke the important life lessons over us and scolded us and gave us endless amounts of sugar are the people we still carry with us, even if the only time we get to see them now is in our dreams or in the memories that dance around in our heads when a smell hits us unexpectedly and transports us to their presence. They molded us and gave us the things we pick up as our torches some nights when things get too dark.

My grandfather regularly drove me to preschool when I was a kid. I'd ride with him to his office and he would do a few tasks before dropping me by the church program I was a part of. We would ride and he would tell me stories about my mom and tell me lies like all dogs are boys and all cats are girls. He would be the person I would call in high school about random things that were going on because I just wanted to talk to someone who wasn't invested in anybody but me. I'd tell him what I was excited about and what I was scared of and he'd tell me things like, "If it don't make your hands sweat a little, it ain't worth doin'"—making me feel like I might just make it all the way through high school without completely deteriorating.

My dad was the one I ran to in eleventh grade when all my friends played a prank on me so hateful I couldn't think straight.

I skipped school, ran into his dorky office while he typed on his half-broken computer, and collapsed into his lap like a four-year-old, crying so hard I couldn't breathe. When things like this happened, he would pray and ask God to make it make sense soon, and look at me and say, "You mean to tell me you let one person tell you that you couldn't do something, and you believed them? Well, I have confidence in you; I know you can do it."

My senior year was blurred with the Great Recession and the loss of loved ones and breakups and family illness. My mom would stop me before walking out the door for school and make me "put on the full armor of God so I could take my stand against the devil's schemes." And I would stand there and roll my eyes and pretend to put on the armor before walking out the door. I'd open my backpack at school and laying on top of my binder would be a notecard telling me everything was going to be okay, with a Bible verse written under it.

My grandmother used to tell me that silk pajamas and pie on Saturday were sure-fire ways to make sure you had a few things to look forward to. She'd take me birthday shopping every year and while I picked out what I wanted she would pick me out a pair of silk pajamas because something in her knew I'd need something to look forward to when all my homework was done. Thanksgiving and Christmas and every Saturday in between that I spent with her, her famous chocolate pie was always available. She knew that sometimes life was harder than it had to be but silk pajamas at bedtime and chocolate pie on the weekends made life more bearable.

My paternal grandfather would show me that life can indeed be lived without a hand. He lost his left one long before I was born, and I never once saw his life slow down. He would make tomato sandwiches with full layers of mayo, black pepper, and salt, and slice his tomatoes thick. He'd point at them and tell me it was my turn to make them for him while he told me that the only people in life who fail are the ones who just lay down and give up. It would take me fifteen years after his death to remember layering that mayonnaise on Wonder bread and those words, which at times were the only words that carried me through a valley of depression.

When my paternal grandmother would call me in my college apartment to make sure I'd received *The Farmer's Almanac* she'd sent me in the mail so I would know when to get my garden in, I'd roll my eyes. But she would be there to answer my questions about growing herbs on the balcony and making homemade biscuits and chicken 'n dumplings. She'd laugh and teach me that cooking in the kitchen is a movement and an understanding, not a strict orderly place with a million rules. You make your own rules. "Hon, you're the captain of that boat."

I know now that I am not strong enough or brave enough or anything enough to get through this life alone. The things that do sustain me are the memories and the words that pick me up when I forget. What are yours? Do you ever stop long enough to remember them? Do you ever notice how sometimes you do certain things and they feel like second nature? It can make you stop and wonder, *How in the world did that come out of me?* Or, have you ever said something to your kid and you don't hear yourself; you hear your mama? That one gets me every time.

As we go through life, we discover our wild, weird, and brave selves, but I've discovered that we also need to pick up the parts of us that were given to us by birthright. The straight talks or the Scripture that you have written on your heart and you are certain you never actually read it; you just have heard it so many times. These memories will nourish us when we don't even know how much we are starving. This is why family matters. The advice and the tomato sandwiches are my foundation, the people and memories that make me who I am.

We can't have the moments that made us who we are without the people who fought hard to do things the way they understood the Lord asked. Fathers choosing to work hard and provide and make space for their families day in and day out. Mothers who laid down their very bodies to give us life, sustain it, and then emotionally nourish us for the years to come. I hope you all have memories like mine to hold on to, and that you are making family along the way that let you know that you belong. These things, these memories, are why family really does matter. Erkles are optional. It feels cruel to know some families don't choose that. But here we are, carrying around the leftovers of their choices. And God, in His kindness, gives us the choice to choose the better way. It's what He intended all along, even if it makes us the mom who isn't as cool.

So, in my own weary, worn-down, grown-up self, I can go through life with my silk pajama sets and bad attempts at chocolate pie and hold onto my value when people tell me I can't do what I set out to do. I buckle up with the belt of truth and remember that everything will be okay while I do something worth doing and I know it's worth doing because my hands are sweating. I make a tomato sandwich in the summer on white bread and I try to do it with one hand and tell myself that giving up isn't an option because I am the captain of my boat. And I do all of it because my family just wasn't very cool. No, they were never cool; they weren't supposed to be. That's what makes them magic.

Classic Tomato Sandwich

(Remember, this is only a summertime delicacy.)

WHAT YOU'LL NEED:

- Your choice of sandwich bread (A classic Southerner uses white bread. I recommend white bread or sourdough sandwich bread.)
- FRESH tomatoes (Preferably fresh from your garden or your local farmers market. Heirloom tomatoes are primo.)
- Mayonnaise of your choice (Preferably Dukes.)
- Salt and pepper

HOW TO PREPARE:

1. Take your bread of choice and, if you have the time, lightly toast the bread. You don't want it too crunchy, just a little golden. Untoasted bread will do just fine.
2. Lather bread in your choice of mayo.
3. Slice your tomatoes to the thickness of your liking.
4. Layer the tomatoes on prepared bread.
5. Add salt and pepper.

Make a glass of sweet tea and enjoy!

CHAPTER 7

Plant Something Strong

*H*e had that Alabama accent that draws out vowels. As the infamous Andy Bernard said, "It falls off the tongue like molasses." He added Rs to words that didn't end in R and some people even got one added to the ends of their names. He was tall and handsome and well-liked by the community we lived in.

My grandaddy was wealthy, a man who built a life for himself starting from working as a boy on an ice truck. He built a successful business and did lots of work with the infamous Armand Hammer. You know, Arm and Hammer. Yeah, that guy. His college roommate was Jim Neighbors, the infamous Gomer Pyle from the *Andy Griffith* show and let me tell you, to this day that is the coolest thing I have ever known. In fact, Gomer would call every now and then to check on his friend. And if my grandaddy missed the call, Jim would say, "Just tell him Gomer called."

He smelled like wintergreen life savers and just a touch of chewing tobacco and I thought he was the coolest. I can remember watching him put on his watch that he'd had specially made with our church logo on it. Then, he would fill his pockets. Change, Lifesavers®, wallet, acorns. I never quite knew why he kept those hanging around in his pockets but he did and I didn't know any different.

As we got older, he and my grandmother started taking us on trips. Big trips that required airplane rides and big luggage. Without fail, every single trip we took he would make an envelope for every single cousin. The envelope would be white with our name scribbled on it illegibly, filled with spending money and an acorn.

I couldn't quite figure out why he gave us an acorn. Maybe because our minds were set on the cash. Either way, I always managed to keep every acorn he ever gave me. I would store it away in a little box in my room and hope that someday I would have a reason for it. I never did.

When my grandmother died, it rocked all of us. Him the most, for obvious reasons. He was one of the strongest men I knew and all of a sudden I would look over to him in church and see tears streaming down his face, his hands in his pockets moving around the change and acorns. Grief took over the remaining five years of his life and now that I'm older, I regret how little I tried to be there for him in that. But after grandmother died, something in him died too.

I sat with him at breakfast one morning only a year after she passed. I learned quickly that he didn't want mindless chatter, but to just be together. So I set down my need to disturb awkward silence and leaned into connection. He sat down that morning and reached into his pockets, pulling out his wallet and a few acorns.

I pointed it out and nearly yelled, "WHY DO YOU CARRY ACORNS AROUND WITH YOU EVERYWHERE?"

"Laura Lou, everywhere you go you gotta plant something strong."

It didn't strike me until years and years later that acorns create oak trees, which are some of the strongest, sturdiest, and longest-lasting trees in the world. And in the South, there are no words to describe their beauty and legacy. They stand the test of time.

Not sure why he kept them with him all the time, but I like to imagine he kept them close so when he reached for his wallet or felt them shaking as he walked to work or when he felt grief so strong he couldn't stand it, he could reach in his pocket and remember what he was still here for. That he was still living, and he wasn't finished yet.

I don't think I have ever thought that my day-to-day boring life was remotely important. I know in the general sense that my life has importance, but I never thought the not-so-glamorous days had value too. But he did. He taught me that if I am breathing, I am valuable and offering something to the world. If I am showing up somewhere, I have the opportunity to plant a strong impression, plant a strong love in my kids, plant confidence in my husband, or plant the gospel to a lost soul.

You were put on this earth to do important things, no matter what. No matter who sees it or notices or applauds you. Even if you don't get to see the outcome, you add value to every moment of your life by simply existing.

So show up, do the work, do the scary thing, do the kind thing, do the right thing when everyone else isn't. Be the person who shows up when you're in grief and in joy. Those two are allowed to be married to one another in the same season. Joy isn't circumstantial; it's from within. Grief is just love with no place to go.

When I go home and see the places my granddaddy touched and the things he did and the moments he marked, I am rocked by the reality of those two worlds colliding: joy and grief. I miss him. His wisdom and his quirks. I notice so much how quickly the people who knew him and loved him and remembered him are slowly dwindling too. But the joy, the unexplainable joy, can show up out of nowhere and remind me of the truth he handed to me for so many years.

He is a part of me. We share the same chin dimple, after all. There are a lot of years where I wondered what it would've been like to have him around years longer than he actually lived. What he would've thought, what he might have said, how he might have guided me through business choices and decisions. I realize that when I imagine, it's just a glimmer of hope and healing, because the joy of his memory floods me. And his little words remind me that there is hope for the future. Not just mine but all of us. Things in life will scare us and hurt us and they'll even make us laugh out loud and, yeah, we gotta cry about it most days.

So, throw a few acorns in your pocket, and remind yourself that you have another chance at another day to do another amazing thing.

Go plant something strong.

CHAPTER 8

Grocery Stores

On a recent trip to Pennsylvania I told a story about my mama. It wasn't much, just one I carry around in my mind to brag on my mama every chance I get. A girl sitting in the circle around which I was sharing looked me square in the eyes and said, "I simply have to live where you live. I want to experience it all. If that is your mama, I cannot imagine what the rest of the South is like."

Another girl chimed in, "I haven't ever been to the South, but I heard people just randomly talk to you and help you, that people don't seem to be in a hurry to get anywhere."

I laughed.

They all looked at me with the kind of eye contact that demanded me to either nod in agreement or convince their assumptions otherwise.

All I could think of was the grocery store. A simple place that everyone, rich or poor, young or old, weird or cool, MUST

GO. We all have to. We all have to figure out what we need and stand in the lines or order online and park our car in its right place for picking up. It is where I have made dozens of new friends in the checkout line. It is where the workers stop and talk to you and ask if you need help and where the old ladies standing in the baking aisle will tell you their secret biscuit recipes if you just stop and ask them.

Once, a man with a piece of legal paper was wandering the store like a lost puppy. My mama, along with five other women, helped this poor lost soul who had been sent by his wife on a Thanksgiving grocery expedition.

I wouldn't say that we are better, that our grocery stores look any different on the inside, but the people who shop there live differently and, to be quite honest, they expect different. They expect good manners and hearts that will help. Trust me, every Southern kid knows that if there is a need that must be met, your mama is going to give you a look and a nod and you immediately know that your job is to involve yourself as a means of helping. "Many hands make light work," as my mama would always say.

Just a year into my marriage, I was standing in line at the Old Cloverdale Winn Dixie in Montgomery. I had approximately forty minutes to get all our groceries, drop them at home, and get back to work. I went at an odd time, so I was certain the lines would be short. My apartment was just a few blocks away and I simply had way too much confidence in my time management.

I grabbed my groceries and ran to the line to wait my turn. Only one lane was open and the girl in front of me had two small children. They were offloading their buggy. The youngest, maybe eighteen months old, was determined to help his mama put groceries on the belt. She was managing a smaller screaming baby and the eighteen-month-old was losing his biscuits attempting to put her groceries up to scan. In the chaos, she finally said, "Okay, you can help me! You get the watermelon." She pointed to her toddler.

He picked up a plastic container of pre-chopped watermelon to put on the line. Grabbing it from the top first, the container popped open completely. The watermelon went everywhere: the crevices of the cart, the floor, the grocery belt, and his clothes. The tantrum escalated and became a bigger scene. I could see the mama's whole body change. She was sinking in defeat, the feeling that she would never be able to get out of this grocery store.

At the time, I was not a mother, just a well-rested twenty-three-year-old who somehow in that moment had enough wits about me to just help that mama out. She was frantically pulling out baby wipes and the cashier handed her a roll of paper towels.

I walked up and grabbed the paper towels from her.

"Just go. I got it from here."

She looked at me and mouthed thank you as she tried to calm her toddler, manage the baby, and pay for her groceries.

"I'm so sorry; I know I'm holding everyone up."

In my mind, I didn't really want to help her, but I could feel my mama in the back of my mind, saying, "Grab those paper towels and pick up that mess. Don't just stand around and watch someone struggle. Get down on your knees and help."

Maybe it was selfless of me to intervene or maybe it was my fear that my mama could see me and might consider spanking my twenty-three-year-old behind if I didn't do anything.

Regardless, after washing the watermelon sticky off my hands, I didn't think of it again.

A few months passed and Cody and I were working at Southern Makers, a big event in downtown Montgomery that supported Southern businesses. We had a small coffee cart business at the time and had been asked to be a part of the event. I was knee deep in taking cards and cash and passing out cold brew and hot drip coffee.

A blonde woman approached our cart. I was moving quickly and not really making eye contact, just prepping as people spoke.

"What can I get you, ma'am?" I said while scooping ice.

There was no reply. So I spoke louder.

"What can I get you today, ma'am?" I said again.

Again, no reply.

I stood up and faced her.

The blonde woman was staring at me and had tears in her eyes.

"Are you okay? Can I help you?" I said again.

"Do you grocery shop at the Winn Dixie in Old Cloverdale?" she mustered out.

"Ummm, yes, ma'am, I do; my husband and I live over there. Why do you ask?" I replied.

She reached over our coffee cart and wrapped me up in a huge hug as she cried and said, "I was the woman you helped a few weeks ago. My son dropped watermelon and you cleaned it up for me. You have no idea the day I was having but you stopped and cleaned my mess. I saw an ad in the paper about your business and that you would be here. I needed to come and personally thank you."

I was so jolted by her hug and abrupt conversation I didn't know what to say. I just stood there and hugged her, making our coffee line twice longer than it would've been.

I don't know that what I did was all that significant; I would dare call it an exceptionally small act that I truly only did because it was how I was raised and, truthfully speaking, my mama put the fear of God in me for moments like that. But when this woman made sure to show up at the same place as me when she recognized my face in the paper just to give me a hug, I realized that a lifetime of being pushed to see a need and fill it was all worth it for that small little moment.

Southerners may have a history that makes us look bad. Some think we are just plain stupid. Some feel frightened at the thought of speaking to someone in the grocery store line, let alone helping them. Some even cringe at the thought of showing up to thank a stranger for what they did.

But for us, it's just who we are.

It took me thirty-one years and a trip to Philadelphia to find out that people don't make friends in the grocery store. I made a comment about making friends in a checkout line and I've never seen so many blank stares looking at me like blinking cursors on a computer screen. I was shocked.

"You never talk to the person in the checkout line?"

"Not unless they are in my way and I need them to move," one girl replied.

Another chimed in, "If someone is staring at me, I tell them to f— off."

My jaw dropped.

I came home to our little town in Alabama and started wondering about every little thing. *Would this happen in Pennsylvania too?* I would ask myself.

I walked into our coffee shop and the barista yelled out, "It's Mrs. Bell, y'all" and the rest of the employees yelled, "We have DECAF for you today! We are so glad you're here!" I left there and passed by a local boutique called Namely Claudia's where Miss Claudia herself was hanging up Christmas decorations. Emmy Lou stopped to say hey and Miss Claudia got off her ladder to hug her and kiss her face and call her things like "Hon and Sugar" and promised her a Sprite® in a fancy glass next time we came to her store.

We got in the car and went into Walmart, where we got all our needed groceries and Oaks—then eighteen months—decided to throw a tantrum. An older gentleman and his wife standing in line next to us picked him up and entertained him while I off-loaded the groceries. They smiled as I apologized and told them they didn't have to do that. They said things like, "Our grandbabies moved away; this is a good moment for us to feel like we are close to 'em," and, "It feels nice to smile at someone who doesn't have a wrinkle on their skin."

We made our way to the post office, where we mailed off a million packages for my business and the postmaster came out of her office to play with my kids. She gave them stickers and suckers and raced them back and forth between other people standing in line to let them play. She knows my kids' names and makes a point to love on them every time we come in.

We made our way home on the back, bouncy roads of New Harmony, weaving between county lines, passing tractors with men waving me to pass, driving along pastures and fields of cattle and chicken houses. To every truck that passed me by, I lifted my hand to wave and always got a wave back. Sometimes a full hand, sometimes just the index finger of the hand that was steering the car.

I arrived home and got my kids down for a nap and I wondered, for a brief moment, if anyone in Pennsylvania gives a one-finger wave.

I might never know.

But I sure am glad it happens here.

These little things, the people, the moments where we remember what our mama would expect of us, the way someone helps you when you are drowning, these are my little pearls. The ones I pick up and start stringing together. They are the shiniest moments, the ones I live for. I want to keep stringing together those pearls. I wanna hear the clickety noise that happens when another pearl is added, another reminder that where I am matters; who I am matters. Whether someone knows me or not, they see me; I belong. I belong so much that my belonging is simply second nature.

I know the lady in the grocery store with her dumped-out watermelon really didn't want her wreckage exposed. I know how awful it feels to have your suffering on display and feel like the whole world is sitting by watching what you'll do next. I want to give off the impression, we all do, that things are going swimmingly. Why do you think we breeze through "How are yous" with "Goods"? Because we want to always turn in our best work and bring home the report card that life is brilliant and we are worth being loved. I'm happy; this is great; I don't feel like I'm drowning every day in this season of life.

But in a season of searching, hunting, stretching, and growing, I learned really quick that the only way for me to put in a good report card is to have watermelon slices spill out everywhere for someone to see. Because most days I do need help. I do need support. I do need someone to grab my hands and look at me and say, "I got it. You keep going; I'll do this part.

I think there is something really sacred about the way this all happens. One-finger waves and grocery stores full of people who help because they don't know how to live any differently. Really, in all of that, we are all coming home to what our mama told us to do. We are all rallying around what it means to belong and to help someone else know that no matter what. They belong too.

PART 3

HEALING

CHAPTER 9

Sometimes We Just Need a Day

I was eighteen years old. It was the fall of 2009, and my boyfriend of two years had just dumped me. We were knee-deep in the recession that followed the housing crisis and my family was suffering under the financial weight of it all. My older sister was battling scary health issues. We were already heartbroken from a conglomeration of sorts and this boy, whom I was certain I loved and would marry, ended it.

To make an even bigger ache, he went to the school yearbook to make sure that we wouldn't win "Most Likely to Be Married" because he was planning to dump me. So a whole portion of my school knew he was breaking it off before he actually did.

Mortified doesn't even begin to scratch the surface of my emotions.

I was getting ready for school, tucking my Oxford button-down into my plaid uniform skirt when my mama walked into my room. She grabbed my hands, tucked a note into my backpack to read when I got to school, and prayed for me. When she finished praying, she went from her soft, kind voice to her stern face, so I knew she was about to get serious with me.

"Now listen to me. You ain't goin' to school and whining and carrying on about him. You're gonna be kind. You will be respectful even if he chooses not to be. You will show him that you know how to behave. You will not gossip. You will not create a scene. You hold those tears until you get to your car after school and then you can squall like a baby. Come home, and I'll cry with ya. But you will go to school all day and you will not call me begging to leave. We are gonna make it through this year and it is going to be hard. But you can do it. Ya hear me?"

"Yes, ma'am" I replied. Knowing good and well that I may have to sit in a bathroom stall after every class period to sob for five minutes.

My parents loved my ex-boyfriend. They really did think of him as their own. And to my surprise, when we broke up, they were heartbroken with me. I just didn't know it at the time. I simply knew my mama was trying to teach me the art of holding my tongue from slander and acting more mature than I was. She knew every class I had with the boy and I knew she would be praying me through each class period until I got home, but I was an emotional wreck.

I went to school and managed to be okay until third period—the first class of the day that I had with him. He sat right behind me. We had picked those seats on purpose that way and the moment I stepped into the classroom I was heartbroken with the knowledge that I would have to sit in that spot until I graduated high school.

The bell rang and my teacher was starting class when the secretary came over the intercom: "Laura Plunkett for checkout, please."

My gut dropped. I was certain that someone in my family had died. It was the pattern of my senior year. Financial loss, repossession, a broken heart, a sick sister, and now what? What was happening that I was being checked out of school at ten in the morning?

I packed my backpack, trying my best to avoid eye contact with my ex, and made my way out of the classroom. When I turned the corner of the hall into the lobby of the school, my mama was standing there. Her purse was clenched under her arm the way she would do whenever I knew her emotions were tight. I was far enough away to see her posture and my gut dropped.

"Mama, is everything okay?" I said.

She nodded and said, "You know, sometimes, we just need a day. Let's go eat fried chicken." She opened her arms up to me and we hugged and stood in the lobby of that small private school in Montgomery and hugged. And I cried harder than I could've possibly cried. Because my life, at eighteen, was hard and confusing. Everyone told me I was lucky, privileged, so blessed, and had everything to be thankful for. But in that moment, my mama knew that I was crumbling under the weight of trying to believe that it was all okay when my heart was broken from within and a stupid boy had just grabbed it and made sure it was nice and shattered.

She took me to Zaxby's, where we split a fried chicken plate we had no business buying. She let me cry. She even let me say bad words that started with F and sounded like suck (we never notified the church elders) and horrible hateful things that had been stirring up in my heart. She let me say all the things about everyone at school that hurt me and how much I hated them. How much I hated being at school with rich kids and how much I wanted to drop out or go back to my old school to finish the year. She let me say it all because it was there that no consequences would happen. Just tears over fried chicken and French fries and an ice-cold sweet tea.

I didn't need rescuing; in fact, I couldn't be rescued no matter how hard anyone tried. Anyways, it wouldn't have been rescue; it would have been running. My life was a big bottle of pent-up tension of being a painfully obsessive people pleaser who, for the first time in potentially my entire life, had no way to convince the boy to change his mind. I had no way to be nice enough to change the financial status of my parents. I couldn't be good enough in a performance to no longer be talked about. I could not do anything. The people-pleasing community will know that we would rather take a ride into glory than face that. I wanted the story to be over, my happy ending to appear, and for everything else to disappear. But I was stuck, smack in the middle of a novel where the reader is trying to decide if they can stick around for the happy ending or if it's just too sad and they should shut the book.

More f-bombs would be dropped, more hurt feelings would come, and there were plenty more days where I thought dropping out of high school sounded more fun. The people pleaser in me couldn't control the narrative. I couldn't please enough people to manipulate the circumstances to swing in my favor. We can't control the story as it all transpires. That work is for the fiction writers and puppeteers of the world. But for our non-fiction lives, it has to be lived.

I wanted to lace up my running shoes and take off, but what I ended up finding after months of change and transition and a few more rounds of fried chicken plates and cold sweet tea was what I really wanted, and needed, was healing. I needed a nurturer to come in and say, "This is the road. You have to walk it." My mom rescued me for a day, but she nurtured me through the rest. I found people and friendships that could help me disconnect long enough to muster the strength for another day, another hard thing flung into the Plunkett household, another long conversation or murmur of gossip that would spill through the halls of school.

Not even two weeks after our lunch, I was at my church youth group Christmas party playing dirty Santa for the hundredth time. Christmas really brings out the joy of giving stupid gifts. A guy in my youth group approached me fired up and ready to argue.

"Go ahead and tell your boyfriend to stop asking my girlfriend out. It's getting old."

"What are you talking about?" I said. "We broke up two weeks ago."

"Yeah, well, he has been asking her on dates for weeks."

My stomach dropped: another punch in the gut, another stupid high school moment that felt bigger than it needed to be.

I ran from the room. I knew everyone was listening. I knew I was slowly becoming a spectacle—not only for being the girl who had been dumped but clearly the girl who had been with someone who'd had very little respect for her for a long time. I hid myself in the church kitchen pantry and sat on the floor.

Our youth minister's wife came in and locked the door. She knelt down and looked at me.

"Laura."

"Just leave; I'll get myself together in a minute," I snapped.

"I'm not leaving," she said as she sat on the floor next to me.

"I'm just embarrassed. Even if school and boys disappeared, it's still too much. "

"Friend, this will not be what breaks you. What will break you is if you miss the Lord in all of it. Don't trade your pain for answers to things you don't really want to know or maybe even need to know."

The conversation quickly evolved into us skipping dirty Santa and laughing and eating five-year-old chips out of the church pantry. The Lord brought me closer to knowing that home can be the place where we break and it can also be the same place that we heal. El Shaddai, the God of the Mountain, the healer and redeemer, and perfecter of our faith, draws us back to redemption, not always from rescuing or helping us run, but by linking arms and saying, "I am not going anywhere."

It would take years before the economy had mercy again and families across America would recover, including my own. It would be just five months later that I connected with and started dating my husband. I would see redemption in every single corner of life for years to come after a season of needing to just be nurtured through the discomfort.

Life would throw new curveballs like chronic pain and infertility and miscarriages. It would throw me into worlds and businesses I never dreamed up and slam doors on careers I knew were the path I was supposed to be on. I know that I am not bold enough or whole or new or shiny or strong enough to do it all and heal it all and see the end before it comes. I will never be able to see fully what I have done right or wrong or who I could've been had I taken one different step in another direction; I can't even see who I am becoming.

The good and the bad and the ugly and the awesome, none of them are bulletproof and no life, no matter how glittery the social media highlight reel, is a fairy tale. But it isn't a scary movie either. It's all just a screen with the curser blinking, waiting for the Lord to type the next word, for the enemy to try to erase the good parts, and for new characters to be added in to nurture you consistently through the hardship and sit on the floors of church pantries and eat old chips from potluck 2005 or drive their beat-up Buick LaSabre to Zaxby's in the middle of the day to eat fried chicken and cry your eyes out.

Because sometimes, we just need a day.

CHAPTER 10

Finding the Post Office

$\mathcal{I}$s it just me or does anyone else feel an immense amount of inadequacy in a post office? As soon as I walk in, I feel insecure about my ability to do the seemingly simple task of sending a package. Always writing the address in the wrong place or accidentally buying packaging for triple the price and having the postmaster gently remind you of cheaper options after you've inserted your card. That's me and has been me for the entirety of my post-office-attending years.

I was struggling one day as I carried a wrapped gift nearly half my size into our local post office. I felt like I had stepped back into 1987; it even had a door that dinged when you walked through it. I had a slew of packages to ship off for my business, along with said gift. I sent off my business packages first, leaving the gift for last. Finally, staring at the beautifully wrapped gift, I caved to destiny.

"What is the best way for me to package this? Do y'all have a bigger box it can fit in to ship?" I grimaced at my lack of knowledge.

The man at the counter stared at it a while and then decided he needed to call in reinforcements. He didn't think they had a box big enough to box up the gift. The next man walked in, gave it a good stare, and then began speaking in a language that I didn't know still existed: small town directions.

"All right, ma'am," he started in an accent that felt straight out of a Hollywood exaggeration. "You got a couple of options here. Number one, you can go back up the road to the Walmart; grab you a bigger box. All them boxes is right next to the technology stuff. Can't miss 'em. Grab you one of them, box it up, and bring it back here to us." I listened intently, hoping that another option would come up to keep me from making my seventy-fourth trip to Walmart that day. "Now option number two is this: Go on up to the Walmart, grab ya a bigger box, package it up, and go to Latham's Pharmacy. It's just right up the road."

A pharmacy? What did this have to do with my shipping options?

"Now, when you go in Latham's, you'll have the pharmacy, the grill where they cook burgers, and then the UPS. Go to the counter and tell them that you are there for UPS and they might be able to ship it for you."

At this point my ability to opt out of Walmart was slipping through my fingers.

"Now ya third option might keep ya from Walmart," he went on. *Glory to You, Father*, I thought. "You know where Burger King is on Highway 231?" I nodded. "Across 231 from Burger King is a pawn shop." At this point, the words "pawn shop" made Walmart sound heavenly. "Now the pawn shop has two doors. One door takes you in the pawn shop but the other door is a FedEx. Now I am not too sure which door is the pawn shop and which one is FedEx but when you go in just ask and they will let you know if you are in the right place. The owner decided to get one put in to help folks ship stuff. Just kinda goes together . . . like salt and pepper, you know?" he finished.

Does it? Does a pawn shop go together with FedEx like salt and pepper? I thought.

I smiled and repeated back his very detailed instructions to make sure I understood him correctly and walked back to my car trying to decide which route I should take. I opted for pawn shop/FedEx because it seemed like the option that would give me the most bang for my buck and honestly, I just didn't want to go back to Walmart.

I took a leap of faith and drove myself to the pawn shop across 231 from the Burger King. The postman was indeed wrong; there was a small FedEx sign pasted to the door, differentiating it from the pawn shop.

Thank you, Lord.

As I write this, I cannot help but laugh. Not necessarily because the descriptions of everything he told me were so random and seemingly absurd, but because there is something so sweet about a small town. But at that time, I was less than a month into moving to this little quaint corner of Alabama, and it had nothing. At least I was certain it had nothing. It didn't have my friends and the only food options were greasy Mexican restaurants and fast-food joints. It wasn't anything fancy and everything felt five years behind.

I felt like I was missing out on life and everything was moving forward without me, like I was trapped in some box and couldn't get the lid off. My days were spent scrolling the internet and seeing what I was missing out on with my friends back home, the events taking place, the momentum of the town. Everything that worked. Everything I loved. Everything that made sense.

I had a hard time making room for a place like this. I knew that making room might mean laying down other things I was holding on to with white knuckles. The past was already gone and the amount I was losing was ticking up by the second because I couldn't bring myself to plant my feet in a place that seemingly had so little.

There wasn't a simple place in that entire town to go and ship my gift, no easy drop off or perfected system. I had to drive all over creation and peek into doors and hope that I picked the right one for FedEx and not a sketchy pawn shop. I remember that day at the post office as one of the most visceral first moments of homesickness.

Memories are stirred up by experiences, places, and tastes. I am such a believer in the power of memory.

Taste memory is simple. It doesn't need to be fancy or memorable. We remember the pot roasts and chicken casserole and rolls and green beans straight from the garden and the smell of charcoal grills that remind us of summers we'll never get to relive again. That's why I love a good supper around the table. The sound of forks clinking or ice hitting the sides of glass cups full of sweet tea with extra lemon. Taste memory is the reason

I make sure there are chuck roasts in my freezer in case I need to throw together a quick meal for company. Because to me, pot roast hits familiarity, a taste memory if you will, of Sunday afternoons with my parents and sisters and grandparents after church when we would eat until our stomachs swelled up to our lungs.

Sometimes, most days, I felt desperate to travel back physically to other places, and other times through the smells, tastes, and flavors because I longed for so many things lost—like holidays I wouldn't get to spend with friends because they weren't my neighbors anymore. Vacations that were once a day trip would now take four extra hours of driving. Pizza Friday nights and favorite restaurants were no longer date night options.

I remember one night, back in Montgomery, just a few weeks after Emmy Lou was born, Cody planned a surprise date night. He had to start traveling for work when Emmy Lou was just four weeks old. I was sleep deprived and socially deprived and everything deprived, so much so he could smell it through the phone three hours away through my mustered up, "We are doing great!" He called my mom and asked her to watch Emmy Lou while we went to dinner at a fancy restaurant five minutes from their house.

When I think about that night and how we slipped away for a quick date and held hands across the table and walked over to Great American Cookie like we were teenagers at an indoor mall again, it makes me reflect on what I do miss and what I really don't.

You see, that three-hour distance we had Monday through Friday is why we moved in the first place. Because for eighteen months we did that and only held hands on the weekends. We didn't have each other to lean on when things got tough because we were so far apart.

Yes, I missed my people and my cousins and people from high school that I would sporadically run into. I missed the feeling of being rooted so deep somewhere that even if I didn't know you, I could find a way to be connected through a mutual friendship.

Oh, but there was lack. I missed my people, but I didn't miss the nights I spent alone in our apartment with a small baby praying that Cody would get off work early enough to come home. I didn't miss our tenants next door writing hateful texts and knocking on our door about their lawn not being cut while my baby was screaming on my hip.

Just after we moved to Arab, I was in a local boutique with Emmy Lou because I knew the owner and she called me "hon" and made me feel like I was part of something.

There was a girl behind me in line. She heard me say my daughter's name and she said, "Oh I have an Emmy Lou." I smiled at her and we exchanged connection. Before she walked out the door she turned to me and said, "Welcome to Arab. I am glad you're here."

Here I am, three years later, looking back on my time spent wandering around town, talking with the chatty postman, meeting people who have kids with my kid's name and realizing that home isn't singular. You don't lose one to take on another. But rather, your world and your heart expand with each new home and set of experiences (even pawn shops). New versions of you pop up and the old ones stay. The precious and tender moments that are occasionally unlocked by the smell of pot roast, the dinging of the post office door, the woman who calls you hon', or the girl who actually looks you in the eyes and tells you she's glad you live here . . . those are the ones that make your heart bigger and bigger, expanding what home can be, making space for the good stuff. The God stuff.

Yes, there is a lack in this town. But I now see it as the good kind of lack. Lacking pretentiousness. Lacking a need for three brick and mortars when you can have a pharmacy, grill, and UPS store all in one. Lacking a care that that isn't the norm for any other town carrying a population of more than ten thousand.

I love that directions involve landmarks instead of road names. That it involves engaging with people to figure out if you're in the right spot AND knowing that when you ask, the next person will willingly take you to where you need to go, without an ounce of hurry in their bones.

The best lack I have noticed in this small corner of Alabama is that not a soul is in so much of a hurry that they can't stop to help someone else. It's the norm. And honestly, it's becoming mine. I am slowing, releasing the spirit of hurry out of my life, by living here long enough to realize what I have missed out on in my old life. For now, I'll smile and giggle to myself when I eat a hotdog at the pharmacy/grill/UPS store before passing the pawn shop/FedEx depot on my way to Walmart.

The girl who had a daughter named Emmy Lou found me again two years later. In Sunday school. I remembered her words; she remembered my face. She won't ever know the moment that etched itself right there onto my heart and made me see the God stuff for a brief moment within my own misery. The memory of that moment drew a road map inside my chest—one that reached from that time at the grocery store to standing in that church choir room. I saw pinpoints where things got better, where life made more sense, where Arab felt less and less horrible and more and more like Stars Hollow. (Yes, a Gilmore Girls reference.)

Montgomery is my home. Arab is my home. And Cody is my home. More than anything, I have learned the hard way what it means to come home to myself, deeper than a location or road map or circle of relationships or shared roots. Underneath all the layers of identity and belonging, laying beneath the connection and the expectations, all the longing and unbelonging, all the crazy routes to find the pawn shop so I don't have to go to Walmart, all my loss and all the transition, I found myself again. I found home.

Sometimes lack is what we need to see what really matters. To find the root of it all. I lacked seeing my husband on a consistent basis. So, I packed my bags and moved to a town that seemingly lacked everything and in turn, brought me home.

CHAPTER 11

Biscuits with Mama Rue

*M*y grandmother—remember, the one who mailed me *The Farmer's Almanac* when I was in college—would often call to check in on my "balcony garden." You know, my cilantro and oregano, basil and rosemary, in little pots I had found at the thrift store.

"It's all coming in just fine," I'd tell her.

"Well, hon, that's all I needed to hear."

When she wasn't in the garden or on her porch, Mama Rue was in her kitchen. She moved in that kitchen without stopping to think or bat an eye or scratch her head. She walked in and the kitchen moved with her, like it knew what she needed before she needed it. I would listen to her telling stories on the porch while she peeled peaches without even looking before making a batch of peach ice cream.

Mornings at her house smelled like cast-iron skillets full of sausage gravy, eggs, and orange rolls. She would pat out biscuits and serve them hot. And those biscuits, they tasted like her. She would put a bowl of butter bigger than my face right in front of me to lather my biscuits with and homemade jelly to add if I wanted it. My dad could try to replicate his mother's cooking, my mom would try to fry things like she did, but nothing ever tasted like hers because, well, it wasn't.

One afternoon in college I decided to try my hand at her biscuits. I was engaged and getting married in a couple of months so I realized this could be a helpful trick to have up my sleeve while we found post-college careers and money might be tight.

"Tell me how to make your biscuits," I asked as soon as she picked up the phone. She immediately started laughing.

"What's got you in such a hurry today, hon?"

"I just think I need to know this for the future." It was as if in that moment it hit me that I didn't know how many more years I would have her. My maternal grandmother died when I was sixteen and I had been certain that I had lots of years ahead with her. Then, before I knew it, she was gone. So, my frenzy maybe was in part panic over losing her and never learning how to make HER biscuits.

"Get you a li'l lard, a li'l flour . . . " she started

"Okay, how much of each?" I asked, ready to write it down.

"Just till it looks right, baby; don't need measurin' cups."

Insert eye roll and a conversation of me begging to know how much salt, how much lard, how much flour to put in and where, and just hearing silence so loud on the other end of the phone I could hear her eyes blinking.

"Hon, just do it till it looks right. You'll know."

I am a do-er, not a lover of just sitting and learning. I want to get my hands dirty and watch someone do something and then go practice it until it is right. And shame can build up quickly when I'm asked to perform without doing something first.

School was a harsh thirteen years of me rarely getting to do and always having to perform well. I should add that I never performed well. It's a wonder I have a bachelor's degree, let alone got into college. The pieces of my education that I actually remember and can still recall today were the few moments when I had a teacher who pulled me aside and let me do it all hands on.

Once, in second grade, Mrs. Castleberry (what a quintessential teacher name, right?) noticed that another girl in the class and I were failing miserably every quiz she gave on perimeter. So, she took me and Alexis (yes, I remember Alexis because this experience marked me and also this girl pulled my hair one too many times during story time) out into the hallway while the rest of the class watched a movie. She had already laid yarn down on the floor and taped it. She had us follow her as she walked the square-shaped perimeter of the yarn. Then she gave us our own yarn and had us make our own squares, rectangles, etc. That was the only math test I got a hundred percent on for the rest of my life.

The older I get, the more I realize that most days we don't get the chance to *do*. We just have to keep going. We live in performance mode, looking around hoping that our performance looks like hers, our hair looks like that, and our kids act the right way (but not too right; that looks weird).

My daughter is starting Pre-K this fall. She is on the waitlist for one place and has a sure spot where she currently is.

The place with a waitlist would be a new location, new classroom, etc. She asks about it constantly because it would be in the same building as her cousin, which is like a dream come true to her.

She asks me about everything. How I would drive her to school, if I could go inside with her, would she know which classroom is hers? Finally, I had to tell her, "You are my first kid. Everything you do for the first time, Mama does for the first time. We have to do this together and learn. We may mess stuff up . . . " She interrupted to help me finish the sentence I so often repeat to her, " . . . but we can always clean a mess and start again." She is content with my answer.

Why is it so easy for her? Start at a new school, try the new job, totally uproot your life and move, try the new hair style, parent the only way you know how the child God entrusted only to YOU . . . why can't that be easy? Or can it? It could be something as simple as remembering that life is about doing and messing up and then doing it all again to see where it can be fixed. But for some reason, somewhere along the way we picked up the idea that it must all be understood the moment we experience it. Perform. Perform. Perform. Make the perfect biscuits the moment you hear the recipe.

I need to know right NOW if it looks right. I need to know right NOW so that I never have to face the part where it all fails. Where someone looks at my work and says it isn't good enough. Where my kid might be the bully at school and I have to face learning how to discipline, disciple, and guide the kid that hurt someone else. Where I try to write a book and it doesn't sell a single copy. Where I attempt a new business idea and I lose money. Nope, don't want to face any of that. I want to get it right the first time.

Why on earth are we so afraid of getting it wrong? We all know good and well that when you spill a glass of milk, the only thing that fixes it is cleaning up the mess, pouring a new glass, and trying to finish the glass before it can spill again. Tears are optional.

I realized that my grandmother may have been onto something. DO it till it looks right doesn't mean the first time. It means the hundredth time. It means every time you make it, the more you do; the more you learn, and the more you learn the more you grow, and the more you grow—well, that's when you get to be the person that someone calls in desperation for a biscuit recipe. And you get to tell them that performance isn't the point of anything with biscuits. It's all about trying and messing it up and being completely okay cleaning up a mess.

A few years later, I was standing in my kitchen on the phone with a friend who had tasted some of my homemade bread and wanted the recipe. It was something I started making to save a few dollars at the store. I was cooking and talking on the phone and my kids were running around at my feet. Everything felt loud but this friend needed homemade bread. She kept asking, "How do I know how much water needs to go in?"

"Just mix it till it looks right," I said back.

"But how long do I bake it?" she asked

"Just bake it till it looks right," I replied.

Her questions kept flooding in. How to know and what to do and what is "right." I stopped. I zoomed out and felt like I was observing myself floating in my kitchen, moving in a way that the kitchen moved with me. I was on the phone telling a friend how to make something by simply just doing it "until it's right." I was moving from the oven to the counter to the sink like my grandmother did. I didn't have to look or think; I just knew. Just like her.

Those phone calls, the ones I made in college in a frenzy, watering my little balcony garden, and asking questions to make sure I didn't miss my moments with her . . . they were all in my kitchen with me. The frantic calls were both a need for her calm voice to soothe me and the panic that came with living my life in performance mode. "If I don't perform well, the love will disappear." This is the lie I have carried around on my back for most of my life. It's why school could never be my stage. I can act, I can sing, and I can dance—and all these things I learned by doing.

Things don't always "look right," whether on paper or in a mixing bowl, whether in the carpool line or T-ball practice, in your new job or new adventure. Maybe it's in your friendship or in your marriage that is hanging on by a thread. Sometimes we pour in all our best attempts and it all burns. To that I say, grab your oven mitts and toss the ruins in the trash and try again; do it again. Do it bad and fragile and hurt and broken and anxious and nervous and devastated and excited. Do it all again.

Do it until you are the one grabbing all the friends that are failing and laying out the straight line of yarn and helping them walk their feet step by step along the edge of all your years of hard work and learning and growing and doing. Just like the Lord did with you. Do it all a hundred times over until you can close your eyes and listen closely for the still, small voice whispering in your spirit: "It looks just right, hon."

Mama Rue's Biscuits

WHAT YOU'LL NEED:

- Crisco®, lard, or butter
- Self-rising flour
- Milk

HOW TO PREPARE:

1. Cut Crisco®, lard, or butter into flour. Add milk by the teaspoonful. Mix it all together till it looks right.
2. Drop dough by spoonfuls onto a greased pan; bake them at 425 degrees till they look right.

CHAPTER 12

Yellow Prom Dress

*T*here I was in the middle of my senior year, dumped and heartbroken and trying to cope with everything else that was falling apart around me. I read my friend's parents' names in the newspaper under those who had filed for bankruptcy and I feared that could happen to my family. In the aftermath of the 2008 financial crisis, I watched the wealthiest people in my life suddenly become stressed and make hard choices to spare their finances. I noticed our pantry felt barer, and that beans, rice, and corn bread seemed to be our staple. I couldn't get my ACT score over nineteen and I was certain I wouldn't get into college. Life was . . . fragile. I was . . . fragile. The thought of celebrating a single thing seemed pointless, because it would all go away anyways. I was young and didn't have the tools to process the heaviness around me. And I know I wasn't the only one.

In the mornings before school, I would get ready and sneak into my sister's room. She would be waking up for the day and I would hop onto her bed and we would gossip or laugh or talk about nothing for thirty minutes until I absolutely had to leave for school. I am certain that during my senior year of high school I was late over fifty times and was only charged one detention. I'd call it mad skills. Those mornings with her were sacred to me. She was older and cooler and had a real job with real money. She had just moved back home after finishing up school and spending three months serving orphans in Morocco. She was legit.

Meanwhile, I was wondering if I needed to just go ahead and start bagging groceries because college seemed to only be for the smart people, the ones who were going places and doing big things. Not for the kid who never had a year of life without a math tutor and spent years barely scraping by with grades. But somehow, someway, through a streak of luck and the grace of God, someone asked me to prom. A story that should go down in some record for the high school I attended as the most romantic prom invitation. Done before the days of TikTok. And done perfectly. I sealed the date but as the day came closer, I knew that my outfit would be a repeat situation.

I was a senior at a private school where the wealth of a lot of the students had kept them secure and capable of having luxuries, like a new prom dress. I pulled my dresses from the years before and called on every girl that was at least five-foot-ten and somewhat wide-hipped to see if they would be willing to let me borrow one so I didn't have to be the girl who repeated a dress. Call it vain or call it being tired of being broke, whichever one, it was me. I didn't mope about it though because, honestly, how would that make my situation better?

My big sister, although living in a season of major transition, had managed to snag herself a new job and made a decent living for herself. She's the brains of the family. I am pretty sure she snagged all the smarts because I knew in my soul I was going to fail anatomy that year. She came to me one afternoon and said, "If you can find a dress you like, I'll see what I can do . . . but it can't have sparkles. Not one ounce of glitter, got it?"

She and I are different breeds. I am tall and extroverted; sparkle is my middle name. She is the short sister whose name is listed next to the definition of introvert. Classy and modest is her game. I decided to go on a hunt to find the perfect dress. My friend and I picked out one that was unbelievably out of budget, and I told her about it when I got home, honestly certain that the dress wouldn't ever make it off the rack.

Weeks went by and our pantry was still beans and rice and cornmeal. When I consider that season, things feel hazy at best. One night, while sitting at the table doing my homework and trying not to fail my anatomy class, my sister walked through the door. In her hand was a garment bag with a yellow BCBG dress: ruffled bottom, strapless, no sparkles. I looked up at her and we made eye contact. She looked at me with a big smile on her face. I burst into tears and barreled toward my sister who hates hugs and nearly knocked her to the ground. Because in spite of her distaste for hugs and large crowds, she has the loudest and biggest love I have ever seen.

There are people in my life whom I strive to be more like. The celebrators and memory makers. The ones who take joy seriously! In my brightest moments, that is who I am. A noticer, a person who celebrates the little moments that often go unseen. It's easy to be that person when life is easy, when the bank account is not thought of and the debt is paid off. It's easy to be the celebrator when you haven't lost someone who was everything to you, and to be the memory maker when no one in your life has become only a memory.

But what about the seasons when you can't keep your head above water? Do we shut down celebration and memory making then? That's when you know for certain that being the celebrator and the memory maker is an art, or rather, a discipline. It's a muscle that has to be strengthened in the warm parts of summer, sweating out the bad to make room for goodness when winter inevitably comes.

I spent my years trying to make sure everyone was happy. A gift and a curse. There's pride that comes with being the happy maker. The one who tries to leave every room you enter with everyone smiling. But seasons will come in life, as they always do, where the happy maker, the memory maker, gets knocked down. There are seasons where I can't quite pick myself up. And believe me, I cry, but then I realize crying doesn't do anything but make others sad too. So, I bottle it up and wait for it all to pass. Most of the time, I do this unknowingly.

I need those little bridging moments; we all do. The ones where that gap is bridged and for the first time in a long time you get to be the one left smiling when the room is left empty. You get to be the one saying thank you and accepting the gift that someone gave you just because, expecting nothing more than a smile on your face.

I wore that yellow dress to prom and I danced and twirled and shook my booty on the boy that took me. (Don't worry, I married him four years later.) I took off my shoes and sat on a swing set with him and fell asleep on his shoulder and thought to myself: *I twirled in a gift. I danced and shook and laughed and thought of nothing sad and I twirled in this gorgeous dress I shouldn't have ever had.* That was the happiest moment that year for me.

We celebrate and we make memories because we have to believe that there are more important matters to attend to each day than what's on our to-do list. We make those memories so that even the darkest times have the sparkle we so desperately miss and crave and want to feel again, so much so we feel it in our bones.

My sister bought me a yellow dress. And in one of the darkest seasons in my memory, that sunshine dress put on the performance of a lifetime in my soul. Marking my memory with celebration to look back and see that we made it to the other side of that season, and we are so much better for it. We were better for the way it strengthened us and more importantly, the way it made us see each other. It healed us in ways we probably only consider when we reflect on the good parts that came from the crummy. Like yellow dresses, just because I have a sister who saw me. Loved me. Cared for me. And dadgummit, wanted me to have a new dress.

I know she told me it couldn't have sparkles, but according to the memory in my soul, it was a straight glitter fest.

CHAPTER 13

I Smoked a Lot of Pot

When I was nineteen years old, I transferred colleges in the middle of the school year. I don't recommend this, mainly because transferring in January is the pits. I feel like warm weather and sunshine brings a little less fragility to the soul. Nevertheless, I transferred and jumped in the deep end of activities so I could make friends and get plugged into a new school.

Faulkner University is a small Church of Christ-affiliated college in the heart of Montgomery. I was back in my hometown and determined that my college experience would not be stripped away because I was so close to home. I spent the semester performing in the Jamboree show; I joined a social club and made friends.

Something to be understood about a small Church of Christ college is that there are a lot of rules. Although it is a sweet place filled with incredible, God-fearing people, the rules are strict. In fact, when I see how many rules have been lifted since 2011, I am appalled . . . also jealous.

Freshman have curfew in their dorms at midnight, all female outfits must be no more than a credit-card length above the knee, and, even if you are of age, there is absolutely no alcohol allowed. The pictures of my outfits in college are honestly hor-rifying. Being five-foot-eleven was excruciating with this dress code, especially when it was a hundred and fifteen degrees out-side, and I was attempting to look cute in a pair of Bermuda shorts. I digress.

At the end of the school year, there was a job description posted for students who were interested in being a church camp counselor/Faulkner representative. I spent my teen years going to church camp and always walked away changed in the best way, so I thought this job might be right up my alley. I went to the meeting for the job and wound up being selected to be a camp counselor. The meeting was very intense.

"You are representing the school. Remember: there is no backing out of these trips. Don't misbehave. Bad behavior will be punished, and if it occurs, the school will take matters into their own hands."

We all understood the importance of good behavior on these trips, mainly because we watched as the school made martyrs out of the students caught with boys in the dorm rooms, kids who were twenty-one and drinking wine, and God forbid, the girl who wore a pair of Nike shorts to class. So, follow the rules: got it. I had no problem. In my head, I would be going to college campuses where youth kids would sleep in dorm rooms, eat caf-eteria pizza, and experience life-changing worship for a week.

Sounds like a heavenly way to earn a buck. To my surprise and, ultimately, my demise, that was not exactly the type of summer camps Faulkner had in mind.

My first assignment was to a small Christian camp in Hamilton, Alabama where I was assigned to ten- and eleven-year-old girls. Not a single one of them wore more than a training bra, let alone knew what college they were going to. It was mid-June and a million degrees in our cabin with no AC. I ate the bad camp food and babysat ten-year-old girls while they fought and screamed about who had let a lizard loose in the room. I wanted to quit the job immediately, but the contract was signed. On to the next, I guess.

The next camp was Back Woods Christian Camp in Lineville, Alabama. I drove there with my male co-counselor who was a nearly lifelong acquaintance. This particular co-counselor had a past that wasn't the most graceful. He had landed himself at Faulkner after a bout of bad choices and over-consumption of recreationals. He was on a good track and making a way for himself. We rode together and talked about pieces of the Bible that didn't make sense and the pieces that we loved. I thought maybe the two of us would have a good week and, hopefully, I would be with kids that were actually ready to go to college.

We arrived at a camp that was a little more than "back woods" and started unloading. I saw a hand-painted banner in the mess hall that said: "Week 4: The Right and Wrong Way to Worship." I stared at it a long time until I realized that was the theme for the week. It was gonna be a long week. The keynote speaker, also known as the old-school Church of Christ preacher, approached me and my counterpart and asked us to sit with him at a table. We had been at the camp roughly fifteen minutes when he approached.

The preacher leaned across the table. "My name is John. So happy to have the two of you here." We introduced ourselves to him and told him we were happy to be welcomed. He proceeded, "Let me tell y'all, I haven't had a drop of alcohol my entire life. No drugs, no alcohol. I am blameless before the Lord in that." He said all this as if he was preaching the gospel. We both looked at him, a little confused, and nodded our heads, trying to figure out the best response to his confession/humble preacher brag. I thought we would just nod and move on, consider a new topic, or maybe end the awkward meet and greet altogether and head to our cabins.

That's when it happened. That's when everything got really, really real. When the Church of Christ blinders were torn down. My co-counselor leaned across the table and started nodding even harder with his approval and connection to this preacher. He started in, "Yeah, man, that is AWESOME. I am so impressed with you. I gotta tell you, though, I have smoked so much pot. Like an unbelievable amount of marijuana and I have definitely been more drunk than I like to admit. But I am healed from that. Hey, saved by the same grace, amen?"

I knew his past. I'd known him since the sixth grade and here I was staring at him, jaw dropped that he had just told this staunch Church of Christ preacher about his weed-smoking days. I knew we were toast, getting sent home to be reprimanded by the school with no pay. But the preacher reached across the table, put his hand on his shoulder, and said, "Amen, brother. Amen." The week proceeded as normal.

My bed was a cot in the loft of an old barn, the preacher preached a topic that is laughable considering the chaotic world we are living in today, brown recluse spiders lingered in my sheets, and I spent the week getting frogs out of the shower. I spent one hour of the entire trip actually talking about the college I attended and the rest of the time was spent scratching my head at theology that didn't make sense. It was miserable and memorable and truly weird.

I still have more Faulkner-themed clothing than I do anything else, but sometimes, just for fun, I reach far back in my sock drawer of memories to pull out this memory. The one where one person who had been so desperately broken found his way back to the cross of grace. He founding healing there and redemption and the guts to keep showing his face when the "perfect" churchgoers could uproot some severe shame. But he didn't care. The shame isn't what he felt, It was grace that carried him, the same grace that saved his soul and everyone else's.

CHAPTER 14

Turning It All Off

I woke up in the middle of May 2022 with an itch. I didn't feel one hundred percent like myself but I hadn't really felt one hundred percent like myself in a really, painfully long time. Our move to the country at the end of 2020, living completely isolated and uprooted from all my community, getting pregnant, having a baby and no friendships nearby and essentially no church family, postpartum recovery, and hustling in my business and an extra job left me . . . well . . . not a hundred percent myself.

The first year, the churches were still closed, and much of the world was still masking their faces out of fear of what form of Covid they might have been exposed to. Within weeks of moving, I found out I was pregnant with Oaks. I had no friends and no church, I was a stay-at-home mom with an online business that I was working tirelessly, and I was painfully sick from pregnancy.

The second year it was postpartum recovery and continuing to hustle for a business that was beginning to sink and I couldn't figure out how to keep it afloat. To say I didn't feel quite like myself would be an understatement. For nearly two years, my life felt flipped. My normal glass-half-full personality began to dwindle down into a cup that wasn't even half empty. It was bone dry. So was my heart. So was my mind. So was my faith. I had crumbled into a version of myself that I hardly knew. I couldn't travel back to Montgomery without crying my eyes out and feeling physically grieved for a week each time I left. I couldn't tell my friends goodbye without feeling gutted.

So no, I wasn't a hundred percent myself. Who would be?

This itch though. It felt like it was coming from my insides. Behind my ear and down my neck I scratched and hoped and pleaded to satisfy this painful unwavering itch. *What is going on back there?* I thought as I clawed at my skin throughout the entire sermon at church. Cody kept looking over at me to see when I would stop acting like a patient in an insane asylum.

"You okay?" he whispered as our pastor preached a vivacious sermon.

"I feel like I want to claw my skin off," I replied. "It's miserable!"

We left church and I spent the remainder of the day trying to get Cody to take pictures of the back of my neck, ears, and throat—and there was nothing there. It was like restless itch syndrome and I was the victim.

The following morning, I decided to take my kids to the gym. They had a pool and I thought it might be nice to get some one-on-one time with Emmy Lou. The past few months had been hard on me and, in turn, I felt like my kids were getting the short end of my stick. I dropped off Oaks at the nursery and I took Lou, who was three at the time, to the pool. We stepped into the water when I felt it. It felt like electricity ran through the nerves on the left side of my brain. The surge was so strong that I nearly lost my balance. The pain disappeared after a few seconds, and I continued playing in the pool with my daughter.

After a few minutes, another wave hit me and this time it was a bit stronger. I felt my vision blur from the brutality of the electric wave surfing the shores of my head. It was the most intense nerve pain I had ever felt. My first thought was that I needed to get home but, sadly, as a mom, my other first thought was that a premature departure from the pool would cause a complete toddler meltdown. *What do I do?*

As a millennial mother, my constant panic is that I am going to do something to leave trauma or some horrifying mark on my child's life. But I realized that in that moment, she needed to hear the truth that something was wrong and I might truly need her help leaving. I looked her square in the eyes and said, "Sister, something terrible is happening to Mama's head. This is a terrible, scary type of terrible. I need you to be brave and I need you to choose to be calm and we need to go home so Mama can see a doctor." Lou looked at me with her big, blue eyes, widened so big I felt like I could sob in that moment. Instead of an emotional breakdown, she grabbed my hand and said, "Let's go, Mama! You have to get better!"

We hurried out of the pool and I did my best to get her dressed and myself dressed between the brutal surges of nerve pain and dizziness. I called Cody on the way home and told him to be ready to take the kids in twenty minutes at the house; something was wrong.

I drove myself to the Main Street clinic in the nearest town.

Surge

Relief

Surge

Relief

Surge

Surge

Surge

"Laura Bell?" the medical assistant called. She ushered me to the back exam room. I sat on the table as another young assistant began taking my vitals and asking me a series of questions.

"Is all your pain on one side?"

"Yes, ma'am," I replied.

She nodded, scribbled on paper, and left me to wait.

The nurse practitioner walked in and began asking me the same questions, looking behind my ears and my neck.

"You have shingles," she said in a very direct tone.

"Absolutely not; you're wrong. There's no way I have shingles. Isn't that for eighty-five-year-olds?"

"Well, hon, you're of the generation that had the chicken pox . . . so it's actually not impossible."

"How in the world would I have gotten shingles?" I asked.

"Are you stressed?"

I paused. *Am I?* I wondered.

I had a constant pang of anxiety racing in my stomach on a daily basis, I was rapidly gaining unwanted weight with a bad diet and lack of exercise, and my joints and face had begun swelling. I would spend my days completely fatigued and exhausted after sleeping eight to nine hours per night. I was working an extra job and I was constantly plagued with guilt that I wasn't doing enough for my kids . . . so, yeah, maybe I was stressed.

"Yeah, a little, I guess," I replied.

"A little stress isn't going to cause shingles. You may want to figure out your biggest pain points because your body is stressed to its limits. I'll write you a prescription to pick up on your way home. Go home and rest. Your body needs rest and relief."

I packed up my things and drove home, wondering how in the world I was going to be able to lay down in my bed and rest. Me? Rest? With a three-year-old and an eleven-month-old? With a business to run? With a husband? With a household to manage? With everything going on? No way.

The following weeks were full of me fighting against all of myself to rest. I couldn't just sit still; I couldn't just sleep. I was so angry that I was being pushed to be still and I resented everyone who tried to make me stop, including my counselor, parents, siblings, and my husband. *I am not a person who can afford to stop,* I thought.

By the end of June, my immune system was tanked and the migraines were beyond unbearable. I was depressed and anxious, experiencing panic attacks that I never knew were coming all while running a business about health and wellness. I was a fraud. I had come to the end of myself. The end or maybe the peak of something deeper the Lord needed me to know. I was stripped down to the bare bones of my identity.

I was a fragile, thirty-one-year-old woman who buried her dreams out of fear of rejection. I spent most of my life living without boundaries so I never had to feel the weight of setting one. I was someone who loved her kids fiercely but, after carrying them, battled severely to love her own body again. I was someone who was walking around in a lonely pit starving for community and afraid of losing it all again. I couldn't bring myself to dive into the community God had put me in because it simply hurt too much; diving in there felt like it was somehow a stamp and seal of final goodbyes to the community I had left behind, the one I had sacrificed for and built life with and joined motherhood with. My old life was slipping from my fingers with every new person I encountered in this new place I called home.

I was angry that my life didn't look like everyone else's, that my Instagram account wasn't going viral and boosting my business. I hated women who bounced back after kids and their family photos looked so Pinterest worthy I could hurl. I couldn't listen to another woman tell me they "weighed less after kids than before" because my self-loathing increased every time I heard it. The business I was growing started to crumble right in front of me. I was crumbling with it. I felt like a fraud and a failure. Like a loser and an overweight, insecure shell of a person who couldn't snap out of it.

In the depths of a panic attack, I heard the Lord ask, "Why can't you just stop?"

In the most Laura form, I asked my husband what I should do. Cody looked at me with a confused look on his face and said, "Why would you ask me what you should do when the Lord so clearly told you? It isn't a question of what; it's more of a question of when."

The fear and panic I felt in that moment sent surges through my body. What will happen to my business if I turn it off for a month? What happens to this life I have been living if I have to set down all my distractions and face the demons that are attacking every ounce of me? I was scared and nervous, anxious about my future and what it would hold. But I did what I heard the Lord say.

I turned it all off. All my social media accounts (my number one source of income). I told all my customers I was stepping back, and I shut down emails and text threads. I stepped back and I decided that facing it all might be the only way to survive it all. I had business partners question my choice and tell me everything I feared. I was turning off social media just as the company was gearing up for summer and my bonuses for social content creation were about to increase. The surging emotion and desire to stay was beyond strong but my burning desire to get back to the person I so needed to be for myself and my family was stronger.

Over the course of the month of July, I spent my days in the garden pulling vegetables. I would feed my chickens and visit my neighbor Maxene. I invited over another neighbor, Miss Betty, to teach me how to make her homemade pickles and I taught Emmy Lou how to can green beans and zucchini. I found my days had more peace and my life felt more at ease.

I met a coach who encouraged me and coached me into the process of writing this book, a dream I set down years ago for the sake of making more money and thinking the world didn't want to hear from me.

I grew up with a father who said to us all the time, "If you make a choice and it turns out to be a bad one, just make a new choice." So I did. For the first time in a long time, I made a choice that was different so that I could find a better one. I hired a doctor to look at what was dysfunctional in my body. I hired a coach to help me rewrite the story I was telling myself for why I couldn't do what I loved. I sweated in my garden and learned to can, which was slow and tedious and methodical. I gave my time back to the things that mattered and said no to the things that stole from my life. I sobbed aloud in my counselor's chair as I processed pain that I had buried so deep over the last two years and honestly, throughout my whole life. I was finally turning off all that should have been turned off years earlier so I could turn on the most important things: adventure, creative work, potlucks, Sunday school and a church family, storytelling and hospitality, and living with an open heart.

As I healed, I learned.

I learned the lies that gripped me and I remembered the true words that sustained me. They were all mixed up in a pile of memories I had to sift through. So, I started turning the sifter. I started remembering the things that have carried me all these years. I picked up the memories that made life bearable, the ones I needed when I first uprooted and moved to this little Mayberry-like town.

I had to learn that things can't go back to the way they were. I would never be going back to the places I missed so deeply, to the people that shaped me and know me and know my people and my middle name and what I was like as a kid. Moving back wasn't what I actually wanted. Even though I was certain it would be my fix.

No, I was learning to find home in myself, in who God made me to be. How He shaped me in my life and in the moments after moving. Where He saw me and drew me back to belonging. Where He reminded me I was safe and that there was hope. It was finding my identity again in who He made me to be.

I believe in the power of Jesus. I believe He draws us back to who He created us to be, no matter how far we go. I love that God created our bodies to tell us when we need help and when we need to slow down, when we need to heal. I love a table set with forgivingness and laughter and take-out and homegrown vegetables. I'll never stop dancing in the kitchen with my husband or giving second chances because Lord knows I need a hundred. I think turning it all off gave me the room to simply remember how much those things mattered to me.

Do I still see the world as beautiful? Yes.

Do I believe that telling these stories matters? Yes.

Am I hopeful for the days to come? Hell, yes.

Since turning it all off, there's an itch in me.

This one hurts less.

It's healing and it's grace.

I'm still scratching.

PART 4
SECURITY

CHAPTER 15

You're Gonna Love It Here

I made my way into the fireplace room for another Tuesday morning ladies' Bible study at the church we were visiting. I liked to cozy up on the back row because I had Emmy Lou in tow and was pregnant with Oaks at the time, and didn't want to feel squished. I can hear all my pregnant ladies nod as they read this.

It was just after the move and I was devastated and lonely and beyond my wits living in the woods with a toddler who didn't care one bit that my world was upside down. Even though it was in the middle of the pandemic, we had been thrilled to find a church that was open and had a mid-week Bible study. I managed to get to it every Tuesday morning at 10:00 a.m. and that was about as social as my life got for quite a while.

I was homesick, morning sick, and trying daily to figure out ways to get my family out of this mess we had decided at one point was a good idea. But I did the work anyways. I waddled into Bible study every Tuesday morning with a bag full of toys and snacks and tried my hardest not to keep driving as far away as possible every week.

There was a girl who came regularly. Petite, bubbly, glasses, kind, clearly loved and adored by the women in the church. Her kids were school-aged—a season I longed for—and she was often the one leading the discussion. She LOVED the town of Arab. It oozed from her, the way she talked about it and believed in it all. *Of course you love it,* I would think. *You've probably been here your entire life, and you have all your family and a million people to call if things get too overwhelming.* I would smile and nod and pretend like I agreed with her, but she saw right through me.

On a fall evening in 2020, I was driving down Highway 231, which runs into Arab. The highway was blocked off; people were walking around the highway with flashlights, and police officers were redirecting traffic. There seemed to be a single-car accident but there was nothing around to show evidence as to why the entire town was out of their vehicles searching for something and leaving their cars to block the highway. I was more annoyed than anything; my trip to Walmart was taking far longer than desired.

The following week, I was sitting on my back row seat at Bible study. This same girl got up to lead the study. She started talking about her love for the town because of "last week's events."

I chimed in, "Are you talking about 231 and the block that went down last week?"

She laughed, "Yes, we sure did block the highway, didn't we?" As she looked around at other women nodding in agreement.

"What happened?" I asked.

"Well, the other night a teenage boy had a single-car accident. His dog was in the car and when the accident happened, it spooked the poor pup, and he jumped out of the open window and ran off. The whole town slowed down and found out what was going on. Everyone got out of their cars to help find the dog, police and everything."

"Oh, well, that's funny," I said sarcastically. But truth be told, I thought it was sweet and charming. I just didn't want to admit that I liked something in a place where I felt so alone.

She looked at me with a big grin on her face and said, in front of everyone, "I know you are sad." My gut dropped. How did she know how sad I was? It isn't like I had voiced it to anyone. She continued, "I know you are homesick; I was once in your shoes. I moved here from Mississippi. But let me tell you something. You are gonna love it here. I promise. It may take some time, but when it happens it will HAPPEN, and you are gonna LOVE IT."

I looked at her and said through tears, "I sure hope so."

I don't know that I spoke to her for another year and a half. That's what happens when you're new and you go to seven hundred churches before going back to where you started.

After hitting year two living in Arab, things began to change. I made new friends. I had a group of moms I went to the pool with on Fridays with my kids. I had a regular coffee date with friends from church. Cody and I hosted a small-group lunch for the Sunday school class we volunteered to teach. Things felt more normal and more routine. I found my pace as a mama of two kids, and I started to feel my health—both physical and mental well-being—restored. My older sister and brother-in-law moved from Kentucky all the way to our farm to live closer to our family and landed right next door to me. Or should I say, "just a pasture over."

I started to learn, slowly—I'm talking painstakingly slow. I am talking more slowly than the hours leading to Christmas morning—realizing that self-compassion is letting yourself end the constant grappling with why and just letting yourself be human and be okay with not knowing how to handle it. Leaning into that allowed me to stop beating myself up so much for not finding the path so quickly and instead taking the long way, because that may have actually been the way I was supposed to go.

That long, winding road that took me around a bunch of corners and curves I couldn't see coming. What I hated was not knowing around each corner if I would find a friend or if I would find more emptiness. I never ever wanted to admit that living here was good because for some reason saying that meant that where I came from wasn't. I white-knuckled my way through days and Bible studies and couldn't allow myself relax into it all. I struggled with my health, and I struggled with finding joy in the moments in between morning sickness and homesickness. I couldn't muster up the courage to give places around me second chances because I was too scared that I didn't deserve them.

Just a few months after moving, I called my mom. I was probably sobbing (please tell me I am not the only who starts to cry the second she hears her mom's voice on the other end of the line). She said something to me that shifted my gaze on my placement and my ability to see this place as well as I could see the place I came from. "Just because someone has been some-where their whole lives doesn't mean they don't need a new friend. Stop believing that you are the only one carrying that ounce of loneliness around."

I remembered that petite, mini-van mom from Bible study. I remembered the way I rolled my eyes when she said that most problems in life could be solved with a table and warm cook-ies, so she always kept a batch of dough in the freezer. I rolled my eyes because deep down I wanted to be the one to solve the problems over cookies. She turned her newness to native-ness and birthed joy from a life where she suffered. She lost, she wrestled, and she pushed back up to the surface—just what I had to do. I thought moving was the worst thing that happened to me, and, for a season, it was, until it wasn't.

You may be in a season where you are clinging for dear life to the things that once were because, for some reason, that is the only piece of yourself that feels safe and secure. Those days are gone. It sucks. You can't go back; believe me, I tried. You have to swim to the surface a little harder and a little faster. You have no other choice. I really hate to break that one to you too. You think you can sulk forever, but you can't. You have to swim. I know, because I wanted to sink and give up a thousand times. But the pressure of the bottom will force you out. You can sink and be forced to the top, or you can swim like your life depended on it and breathe a little faster. Either way, what is down in the well will come up in the water. You'll spew it out everywhere you go if you don't just sit down at the new table over warm cookies and spew.

Trust that people are actually really good. People who promise you and assure you that hope is absolutely around the next corner are actually telling the truth. Somehow, we forget that, even though it is promised a thousand times over in Scripture. We sulk and we judge, and we cling to the past and we roll our eyes at the people who tell us that the world we landed in is actually a good one worth living in. But once we sit down with those warm cookies, we realize the hope against all hope was waiting for us all along to pull up a seat at the table and take a bite to see how sweet it is.

After my sister and her husband moved to town, we took them to church with us their first Sunday and I ran into that girl. Yep, little Super Mama was there as usual. I stopped her to introduce her to my sister, to get some connection going. She was kind and inviting; she shared how her kids were the same ages as my nephews. She turned to me with a glowing look in her eyes and grabbed my hand, "So, do you love it here yet?"

I nodded. She smiled, squeezed my hands, and walked to find her seat. I settled into the pews, my sister and brother-in-law beside me. The music started and I leaned over to my big sister and said, "I promise. You're gonna love it here."

CHAPTER 16

I'll Always Come Get You

If I scream, nobody will hear me. What if I wash my face and on the last pat of my dry towel, I open my eyes to a murderer in a scream mask standing in the mirror? Where do I hide if someone breaks in? What is my escape route while said imaginary burglar attempts to steal my TV?

I'd like to say that by the ripe age of thirty-one I have relieved my life of fear and nervousness, that my bravery solidified the day I graduated high school and moved out of my parents' house. I have had zero trauma in my life regarding burglars and I have never had to face a life-or-death situation. But to this very day, I still check every room, closet, and behind every shower curtain to be double sure nobody is waiting for me to drift into REM cycle so they can slice me to bits.

We spent the first two weeks of January 2023 sick and sleep deprived. The four-day fever, as we deemed it, crept into our house and stayed, along with coughs and runny noses and diapers. I was elbow deep in sleep deprivation and my gag reflex was strengthening with every diaper I changed.

We aren't a family of normal, eight-to-five jobs, which helps in these moments and yet sometimes makes things feel even more emotional. In this particular season, Cody and I were renovating a new investment property three hours from our home on weekends and carrying normal schedules in the week. We had planned to go out of town to work on this project and leave kiddos with grandparents for a time while we knocked it all out. Sickness said no to our together venture, so I stayed back to make sure the babies were brought back to 100 percent health.

This particular Saturday, we turned a massive "no fever for twenty-four hours" corner and I had never felt so excited and relieved. My mother-in-law, who is a nurse, told me to go ahead and bring the kids to her house for bedtime and I could head out of town early the following morning to get a late start helping Cody with the renovations. After a full two weeks of caring for sick babies, crazy fevers, and inconsistent sleep patterns, I managed one evening, by the grace of God, to have my entire home to myself. I gladly dropped off the kids and went back home knowing I would get a solid night of uninterrupted sleep. *Praise the Lord,* I thought.

My parents, whose driveway is a thirty-second commute from my own, said I was welcome to pack a bag and come stay with them that night. In my stubbornness, I told them I'd be fine. Besides, I needed to pack, clean the pile of four hundred dishes in my sink, and get the kids' rooms back in order. My dad nodded to me that evening and said, "If you need me, just call me. I'll keep my phone close." *Need you?* I thought. *I have a silent home that I will leave spotless. I'll watch a Hallmark movie, eat supper in sweat pants on the couch, and turn in by nine.* (In case anyone is wondering, this is every young mother's dream. A night to herself, uninterrupted meals, and silence. A treat I never thought I would wish for.)

Our homes—mine, my sister's, and my parents'—rest on one of our eighty-acre plots. We are close, but if I scream nobody can hear me. That was the thought that started running through my head after my house was cleaned and my dinner was finished. I lay on my couch with tired eyes and watched a Hallmark movie to try and get my head in a place of peace to go to sleep. I even took unneeded melatonin so I would sleep deeply. I turned out the lights, alarmed my home, and got into bed. Then I heard the creaking.

When I was almost in a deep sleep, a toy in my daughter's room fell off the shelf with a bang. I am certain in that moment that my heart disappeared into the lining of my gut for a brief period of time. I remember as a kid my grandfather used to tell me, "If you think you hear someone in your house, get quiet; their adrenaline will be rushing and you'll be able to hear them breathe." I sat up in my bed in silence to see if I could hear someone breathing. All I could hear was my heart beating louder than the drummer boy in my ears. I grabbed my phone: 11:45 p.m. I had to leave town by seven the following morning. I swallowed my pride and sent my dad a text.

Are you still up watching TV? I am having a hard time sleeping and I may be reconsidering my decision to stay.

Do you want me to come get you? he replied.

In that moment, I wanted more than anything to just grab my keys and not inconvenience my sixty-five-year-old father. But there I was sitting in the middle of my dark bedroom—a grown, thirty-one-year-old woman, wife of eight years, mother to two children, believer in Jesus—and I couldn't get the bravery to get my car keys and walk outside to my car.

I could not do it.

My heart was racing.

What if I walk outside and someone grabs me? I'm a goner.

I needed the relief of seeing my dad's face and running quickly to his truck so I could feel safe. He used to tell me when I was little that if I got scared at night all I had to do was holler at him and he would be right there . . . and he always left the light on for me.

Maybe, I texted. *I hate to admit this, but I am so scared.*

Okay, I am headed your way.

I grabbed my pillows and cell phone and water bottle and stood in the middle of my living room, waiting for him to get there. My dad, a true Southern man with farming in his blood, drives a Chevy Silverado 3500 Dually, run on diesel and sweat. You can hear it from a mile away. I stood there until I heard the roar of his truck as he accelerated down my driveway. I set my alarm and slipped on a pair of flip-flops to walk to his truck.

I got in and felt like I had my proverbial tail tucked between my legs.

"Did I wake you up?" I asked. "I really am sorry."

"No, I was just turning out the lights around the house. I had just finished my show." I knew immediately he was lying and that he gotten himself out of bed and dressed to come get me.

"I am sorry I didn't come sooner. I didn't think I would get so scared." It was weird how much it bothered me that he had come to get me at midnight. I felt so horrible for inconveniencing him.

He stopped his truck and looked at me with intention in his eyes. I could see them clear through the reflection of the headlights. His trim hat faced me and he said, "Baby doll, I don't care if I am eighty-five years old and carrying a cane; I will always come if you call me. I am here always. Ain't no need to be scared when your dad is so close."

I nodded in understanding, and we immediately started cracking jokes and making bets if my mom would fuss at me for not just coming in the first place or if she would be already completely asleep. I got to the house and crashed in a guest bedroom and found myself waking up to the sunshine and a stiff shoulder from not moving the entire seven hours, since I had collapsed into bed from two weeks' worth of sleep deprivation. The sleep was sound because I knew I wasn't alone; someone would hear me if I called out and would be there to tell me that everything was going to be okay.

I told a group of friends that story and they talked about how kind and cute my dad was for doing that and saying those sweet things. One of them chimed in, "My dad would never do that or say that to me." My heart sank. *Shame on that dad,* I thought to myself. *Shame on a man who has a child and doesn't show up.* My heart was captured quickly in that thought as I heard so clearly the Lord speak to me, "Some fathers show up, some fathers bail. But THE Father never fails to be there."

I am not sure that I will ever change. I may find myself giving my dad a call when he is eighty-five and I am fifty-nine and too scared to sleep by myself. At this rate, my fear of toys falling off shelves and axe murderers waiting until I wash my face at night doesn't seem to be disappearing any time soon. I don't know about the next seasons of life or the days that are so close that my calendar has the plans marked on them.

Jesus came to a world full of orphans and simply revealed one pivotal truth: that what every single one of us needs the most is a Father. The tragedy in all of it is that this wonderful revelation tends to get buried under the broken condition of our present family culture. So many have suffered under the abuse and neglect of their biological fathers, the wonder of this unmatched miracle is often lost.

Almost every single one of us would be completely healed and set free if we grabbed hold of this revelation. Jesus came to turn our gaze toward a Father who is good and wants to be there at every corner and every obstacle, waiting to cheer for us on the good days, sustain us on the tragic, and rescue us when we veer left on the path clearly marked for us. I hit a point where I realized that if I can truly say "our Father" each week while warming a church pew, I can no longer go around the rest of the week acting like an orphan.

I heard pastor Bill Johnson say once, "Every action and every word in Scripture points to a perfect Father, one who is completely good. When the disciples thought children were not quite as important as the adults Jesus was ministering to, Jesus corrected them. Children flock around good dads. On top of that, parents entrust their children to good dads. Jesus simply illustrated this phenomenon that took the disciples a while to catch on to. He was manifesting the Father to people and the children saw it before most."

But here's what I do know; here's where I land: the Father is always close. His phone is turned on loud and He isn't too tired or too scared to walk out into the darkness to grab you up and take you to a place where peace is so present it feels like sinking into an old, comfortable couch. That's what we all need. The knowledge that, when everything else fails—the people, the job, the circumstance, the relationship, the money—there is a good Father just waiting for us to call so He can help us get a good night of sleep to face another day. One that is full of new mercies for us to see SO CLEARLY.

May this story of my irrational fears be the stark reminder that there is no fear when we rest in the commitment of the Father to come and get us, knowing He will rescue us from burglars or bears, singleness or sickness, homesick hearts, or hangovers with a side of shame. He will always come.

And some days we may not think He will. We may stand ashamed in the middle of our living room, knowing good and well our behavior is not sane or rational—but, then, His love for us isn't either. It makes no sense, which is what makes it so good. And just when we think we may have to turn around and go back to bed and tough it out, we hear the roar of the Lion of Judah blazing through the thick, dark of night to pick us up and carry us to safety. Because that's who He is. A good Father with good gifts who loves all His beautiful, scared, broken, imperfect kids.

The weight of our sin and brokenness cannot hinder His heart to pick us up and take us home. Maybe next time I'll get in my own car and drive myself. But it sure is nice to hear the loud roar of the Father coming to get me.

CHAPTER 17

Maybe We Haven't Lost It

When I was little, I used to wake up in the night in our little yellow house in the country when I would hear the roar of the train go by. There was a track we crossed to get to our home and no matter how far away our house sat from it, I could hear its roar in the night. Most nights I would wake my sister, who would tend to roll over and tell me to ignore it, or I'd scramble down the hall to my dad's side of the bed and tell him I was scared of the train. Some nights it felt so loud that the windows would rattle. Or at least in my imagination they did.

Before I knew it, the train would be gone and all I could hear was the sound of silence enveloping our house. And maybe my dad snoring and my mama telling him to hush with a whack to his face. The silence was so quiet it was palpable, and we all drifted away in it. I'd fall asleep and dream about the ocean or flowers or performing on Broadway as Millie in *Seven Brides for Seven Brothers.*

I miss the stillness. Life that landed right on the cusp of us losing our freedom to phones without cords. It seems nearly antique in our noisy, intruding life. An all-but forgotten thing of no real value, like Morse Code. My generation remembers it and are quick to forget it. They call us millennials; some of us even land in the "geriatric millennial" group. We remember the silence and the lack of devices, but we aged with their explosion into society. We remember and often grieve the way life once was simpler, and things felt safer. But as soon as we remember, we look down to the device that helped us remove the pain or nervousness, without deep breaths. We often act as if a little quiet or peace is a bug that needs smashing before it disappears into the abyss.

In restaurants we have games and shows. In the doctor's office waiting room there's a judge deciding custody for two mishaps for people who shouldn't be allowed on TV. At the oil change place I sit and listen as politicians willingly appear with Tucker Carlson to get publicly raked over the coals. Airports are full of Air Pods and blue light and devices and cords re-charging phones that are already dead by 9:00 a.m. At any given moment, emotional eye contact is at war with the infamous ding of the iPhone or the alert of the Apple Watch. It knows our heartbeat and the threat of sickness before we do, because God forbid we stop and listen to our body long enough to ask it what it needs.

My dad wakes in the mornings at 5:00 a.m. He stumbles his way to his bathroom, showers, gets fully dressed, and then makes a pot of coffee. He sits with his coffee and his wristwatch that has no blue light effects. His coffee in his hands, he sips his coffee, shuts his eyes, and breathes. He does it again and again until 6:30 a.m. hits. Then, he gets up, and goes to work.

Cody and I lived with my parents for eight months while we renovated a house and set it up to move into it. Every morning while I read my Bible, scrolled Instagram, drank coffee, and checked my Google calendar, he would come in and do this sip-and-breathe thing. Finally, I asked him one morning what he was doing.

"Are you sleeping between each sip?" I asked him one morning. He laughed.

"No, I would be snoring if I let myself do that."

"What are you doing, then?"

"I am looking at my day. At each part I see, I am asking the Lord to be a part of it."

All he had to do to see his day was to look at the back of his eyelids. I miss it. The bedrooms without television and the TV not staying on past the Saturday-night episode of *Dr. Quinn, Medicine Woman.* I miss the way the train swept through our little country corner of Alabama and didn't compete with anything other than the sound of my dad snoring.

I've started watching the night come. It really has been a game of watching how long until time changes and I can stay outside with my kids past 5:00 p.m. I like it here. It's quiet. And still. The more still I get, the more I noticed how still things no longer are. I do hear the sounds of my distant neighbors yelling at the dogs or target shooting on Saturday morning at 6:00 a.m., but how do I walk over to their house and tell them they are messing up my stillness?

I miss the way we all used to look at each other. Where the only thing begging for our attention was the call of someone else's voice telling us to come home because the sun was going down. I miss the way we used to tell each other our plans at school and meet up in that spot just a few hours later. I miss how parents even forgot their kids at church or school because they thought the other had them and there was no way to know until you got home. Stillness, silence, and phones with cords gave us a freedom to see clearly, without blurred vision or understanding.

It makes me sad enough to wish for a bad-weather day, where we curl up at home and watch the weatherman till the lights flicker and we get still to see where the clouds are rolling. The darkness rolls in and all of the sudden you get a house full of good, old-fashioned silence. No hums of computers or TVs or baby monitors or the extra deep freezers in the garage. You're free from all the man-made noise that takes away your human-ness. You're still enough to hear the Lord and ask Him to be in that moment or the moments to come. Where all you have to do is close your eyes and see it.

A couple of weeks ago, I went to Montgomery to work on a house that Cody and I have invested in. I was knee deep in book writing and navigating what chapter I would write next and how it would all flow and work within a theme. I told Cody I needed an hour or two to go find some inspiration. I honestly didn't know where I was going to go but I went anyway.

I grabbed some lunch and started driving down familiar roads. I looked for memories at every place I landed. I drove through the parking lot of a church building that my home church once owned. I cried a little when I saw how poorly it was kept. I drove down the highway by that old building past Montgomery Mall, which is now a forgotten wasteland of the city. I remembered the days when everyone talked about a new mall opening.

The path past Montgomery Mall took me to the highway that spit me out on that piece of land where we once lived, a small piece of property where our little yellow house sat, just half a mile from my grandparents' old home. I drove down to see if I could remember where the driveway was or if the house was still yellow. I turned into the drive and found the home still there, the trees we planted towering over it and blocking the view.

I did a three-point turn and made my way back toward my grandparents' former property. I wanted to see it, to feel something, but nothing was coming up. The grief that was once was there was now gone.

Its tan paint was faded and the places that were once bursting and thriving were now dilapidated and broken. I turned into the entrance of the driveway. The fence line was hanging; the weeds were growing over the top of the entrance posts. The driveway was long and I couldn't see far beyond the mess. I felt awkward driving down someone else's driveway just to get a glimpse of a home that might break my heart one more time.

I put my car in park. I sat. I stared. I breathed. And I realized I probably was hitting a wall that couldn't be broken down. As I put the car in reverse and started to check for traffic coming down the two-lane country road, I heard the sound of a train horn. It blew so loudly it startled me. I jumped. I put my car back in park. And I remembered the days that once were, the good ol' days that I didn't know were incredible until I was a grown adult wishing for just a moment to experience them all over again. The boisterous, booming horn pierced through the grief and gave me hope. I could finish the book. I could indeed remember the good days despite the dilapidation of that day.

We can have it all back, you know? The silence and the sufficiency of life without the extra. The extra is fun. The extra captures the moments we are experiencing, sometimes too much. The safety and security aren't in all the stuff. It isn't even in the memory of it all. The safety is in the moments where we close our eyes and ask the Lord, "Will You come into my plans today and do with them what You will?"

Stop. Sip. See.

Lord, will You come for my kid who is panicking about today?

Stop. Sip. See.

Lord, will You help me with my marriage? Show me how I can love my spouse well today?

Stop. Sip. See.

Lord, will You show me how to do my job today in a way that alleviates the stress?

Stop. Sip. See.

Lord, will You give me a moment to share the gospel with someone today?

Stop. Sip. See.

Lord, will You give me the work to do to earn the money that's needed today?

Stop. Sip. See.

We can disappear in the busy; we can blur out the silence with the sound of the latest TikTok trend. But will we stop, sip, and see where the safety really lies? In the small, still moments with the Father. In the small moments with Him are where it all is and, honestly, where it always was.

Have you ever stopped to wonder if the best memories of your life were prayed for long before you ever lived them? Have you ever stopped and wondered: had someone not decided to pray and take God at His word over your life that it may have never come to pass?

What will happen when we stop, sip, and see the beauty that is before us when we hand the safety, the healing, the belonging, the hope, and the identity all back to the One who holds it all anyway? It's too good NOT to see. Maybe sometimes it takes the grief of it to put the car in reverse, stop, and hear the sound of safety reminding you that He was there all along.

I have two kids, so my sleep is intermittent. Now I wake in the night to the pitter patter of footsteps running to my side of the bed to cuddle up with me and see that even though they were in the other room, I was still here. Maybe we haven't lost it after all.

CHAPTER 18

Sisters, Cousins, and Gut Punches

I am the youngest child in my family. Girl number three in our all-daughter household. There were eight of us cousins in total, and I was the runt. We lived near all my cousins and my maternal grandparents, and life looked a lot like trying to keep up with that crew, getting left out frequently because I just wasn't big enough to do what they did. Oddly enough, I'm taller than all but one of them now. Joke's on them.

I am labeled by the Enneagram gurus a Type 2: people pleaser, outgoing, easy to connect with. I was the kid that lived surrounded by cousins and friends and church and grandparents; my inter web was strong, safe, and secure. I didn't know it, but it was. I lived on land that was connected to cousins and grandparents, hay fields were my playground, and fully stocked ponds (not just one, but multiple) just made sense

In all my years of chasing the big kids, I never thought the big kids saw me. I hung on to the identity of being their "kid sister or little cousin." In each school I went to, I was someone's younger something. Was I seen? I didn't think so. I was just the extra pinky toe that they all were surprised was there.

We did life together at every angle—baseball, softball, dance, cheer, church. It was our life to be picked up by aunts instead of Mom, or carpool to church because someone had piano lessons at the same time. There was a period of time when my aunt would drop off my sister and cousin for piano lessons and we would run errands together. Just me and her. She always had Hot Tamales in her console, and I pretended to like them as she shared them with me.

Church was where my friends were mine; my age gap separated me from my familial identity and I was able to run around with kids my age, never left behind, always a part of it all. One particular Wednesday night, a girl at church felt some frustration with me over the vending machine. The memory is now blurry, but we were in fifth grade, just the step before entering into the youth group—a season of the true excitement of being an official "big kid." On our way between the fellowship hall and the sanctuary, this particular girl released her rage, turned to me, and punched me in the gut, the type of hit that leaves you gasping for air and thinking somehow you can reach for it. I stopped, standing in the church courtyard, unable to think straight.

What do I do? I couldn't hit her back; I'd get in trouble for fighting. If I cried, everyone would laugh. If I ran, I'd look scared. I just stood there, backing up and reaching for breath while the group of girls I was with all ran away.

My dad found me in the church courtyard, crying. He couldn't get a word out of me so instead he just carried me and placed me in the back of our family Suburban. My sisters turned to me with a look of concern. "What happened to you?" they asked as I sobbed in the back seat. I mustered up the courage to let them know what had happened and that I was weak and unable to fight back because I was a coward. In my memory, nobody said a word.

One thing to note when dealing with a big Southern family is that you must never mess with a big Southern family. Ever. Because, where there is large, there is Southern. We are indeed the sugar-coat society, where we bless hearts and often pick up rugs to sweep. But what is also Southern is a kind of mafia mentality; it involves girls who are forced to sponge curl their hair but who will ruin your life if you step on the wrong toe of the wrong sister. This girl stepped on the wrong toe of my middle sister, and at this point, all bets were off.

The next Sunday I had to face everyone who had witnessed the disagreement, and I tried to act unfazed. Sunday School went as planned and full service seemed to be the same. At the end of service, I walked to the back of the church to find my parents and make sure that a hearty lunch was happening quickly because we all know there is no hungry quite like Sunday hungry. That's when I saw it.

I saw my sister, huddled with three of my cousins, surrounding the girl who had punched me in the gut. They towered over her and my sister, a fourteen-year-old spitfire, was red hot and ready to fight. She looked her square in the eyes and said, "You touch my sister one more time and you aren't just messing with her; you're messing with all of us." She motioned her finger to the cousins who stood in defense of me behind her.

That's when it hit me. They did see me. All those years of living in the shadow of their moves, staying home while they went on trips I wasn't big enough to go on, of the dance practices that ended in teachers telling me to get help from my sister and cousins . . . they saw me. And I loved it. I loved that entanglement of relationships, a sense of being known and deeply taken care of. Of being the center of a bulletproof circle of safety and history. I reveled in it. A lot of things happened to me the remainder of my childhood, but the gut punches in the church court yards, they ended there.

PART 5

HOPE

CHAPTER 19

On Infertility and the Truth

$\mathcal{I}$ used to have a coffee company, one that sold and distributed coffee beans to different restaurants around the city. Our coffee roaster was hosted in our church building and I would spend a lot of afternoons there roasting coffee and watching Netflix. One afternoon, I was driving toward the church when an extreme pressure came over me. It felt like I had been knocked down by an ocean wave and couldn't get back up. The intensity grew and grew and as it did, my vision started to fade. I could feel my body going into fight-or-flight mode and I was about to pass out at the wheel.

I managed to pull the car over and call Cody. He was working on a job and couldn't really hear me. He kept saying, "Are you okay? Is this an emergency?" Our call got disconnected and instead of attempting him again, I called my mom. She rushed over to me and sat with me as I recovered. I called my doctor and asked him for help and was told to go home and take a Tylenol; they would see me in two weeks.

Lovely.

So, I did.

Within two weeks I was sitting in a chair in their office, receiving the glowing and riveting ultrasound that no non-pregnant woman wants to receive. The ultrasound tech said no words, left, and the door stayed shut for twenty minutes until a woman in a white coat—who was not my doctor—walked in. She introduced herself and began explaining to me that my doctor was in a delivery but would be in shortly because my ultrasound results were emergency surgery results.

Time stopped. I listened to her as she explained words like endometrioma and cysts, ovarian torsion, and endometriosis. Then, my doctor rushed in and looked at my results. He looked at me and offered a prayer and then proceeded to plan my surgery for the following day. They tried to explain to me that this happens all the time and that women suffer from endometriosis every single day. They told me I would have to immediately try to have kids because I might not ever have children if I didn't try to conceive between surgeries. They were pointing and sharing and giving me the I-feel-sorry-for-you-eyes that made me want to sob.

I knew where this was going. I had other family members with this diagnosis, and I knew that surgery after surgery, pills, and everything else in-between would be in my future. And I didn't want any of it. I didn't want to feel like I was racing the clock for kids. I was only twenty-five.

I got into my car and started driving. I didn't know where. My go-to after any invasive kind of doctor's appointment was Chick-fil-A, where I would drown my sorrows in a small Dr.

Pepper and large fry. On my drive I did what any little sister would do and I called my sisters. I cried and carried on; I told them everything that was happening and how I didn't know what to do. They listened as big sisters do.

My middle sister, the feisty one, the one who will gut punch any person who tries to cross her people, listened to me the way that I needed. "They said I might not ever have kids. That even surgery probably won't fix what's wrong. They said I can try but the likelihood is slim." My words were quick and sharp and brief before she was able to intervene with just a few words.

"You're gonna have a baby, Laura."

"What? You don't know that. This is what the doctor said."

"Laura, you're gonna have a baby. Just because they said it doesn't make it true."

I stopped and let her tell me all the ways I needed to get calm and focus on tomorrow and not let some doctor who had seen seven hundred patients that day tell me what would and would not happen for my life.

I would end up having the surgery and trying for ten months to get pregnant before more cysts and more pain and more pressure would return, and another surgery would be booked. It would be surgery, recovering, trying again, and failing again. Finally, I landed in an office with a sign that said, "Let's make miracles happen," with shots in my hand and a calendar that marked every single moment of my cycles. I would go to baby showers for people who accidentally got pregnant, and I would hold in my tears until I got into the car.

People would ask me why Cody and I didn't have any kids and I would pretend like it wasn't killing me inside. I would drive every week to doctors' appointments and put shots in my stomach and hope and pray that I would be able to one day bear a child. It's funny how I remember all those moments where I thought nothing would happen and then a small, singular sentence would interrupt the doubt. My sister. Her words would cut through the walls of despair and tell me that hope was waiting around the corner of the next shot, the next negative test, the next appointment, with a new approach. Her words would linger and sing while I was being poked and prodded and told what to do next.

I remember when my grandfather passed away. We were all at a loss for words. We didn't know what to do or to say; we didn't have the answers or the understanding of how a man could play in a tennis match one week and be dead the next. It all happened faster than we wanted it to. At his visitation, they let the family see his body and say goodbye before any guests arrived to give condolences. The church played worship music while we saw him and said goodbye. This side of my family isn't exactly emotional. They don't let it all flow like my other side of the family. I didn't inherit that trait. My feelings aren't even worn on my sleeves; the face takes good care of that.

I saw his lifeless body lying there and we all went to sit in the seats and wait for people to arrive. I sat alone. I wasn't married at the time. I sat alone in a corner, sobbing in a way I hadn't since my grandmother passed. The loss felt too big to grapple with. I buried my face in my hands and sobbed harder. I felt someone come and sit down next to me and hug me with a force that said, *I'm right here.*

I leaned into the arms. They felt familiar and I knew it was her. My big sister. She wrapped me up and held on tight. The hug said: *It's gonna be okay, you're gonna get through this, this isn't forever, we will see him again.* No words were spoken, just connection and a hug that said: *Hope is coming. Hope is coming. Hope is coming.*

Walking through infertility feels like being lonely in a crowded room. Like grief when you lose someone close. You feel it, but for someone you haven't ever met. You hope and you dream and you pray and you hold your breath every month wondering if the test will be positive or if you'll have to go sit in your corner alone and weep. My people knew about it, the ones I was close with; they knew the weight of what I let them see.

But there were days where I couldn't let anyone in. I needed to grieve and feel angry and throw things when the next pregnancy announcement popped up on my feed. I would walk through my crowded rooms and hold on for life in the waiting game I was experiencing. And I would go sit in my corner and close my eyes to sob, only to feel the arms of my sister wrapped around me and her words, "You're going to have a baby; just because they said it doesn't make it true," ringing in my ears. It would play over and over on repeat to remind me hope was coming. It's right around the corner for me.

Hope itself is right around the corner for you too. Infertility, like other forms of suffering in this life, is a mountain that often times feels too high to climb. It takes the wind right out of you, like falling off the monkey bars flat on your back. And the thing about falling off monkey bars is that there are people there who want you to get out of their way, quickly, so they can have a turn, and there are people who come to see if you're okay and grab you by the arms to help you try again.,

The question about hope amidst hopelessness is, *How in the world do you keep on moving forward when you wish you were on a different road?* The details of the circumstances for each of us may be drastically different, but the need to be brave remains the same. We all have the unbelievable need for courage. There are battles we are fighting after losing a whole slew of others and we are weak. We are weary. We are tired. And we need to know that hope, maybe, just maybe, is around the corner in the form of a win.

I learned with all the shots and the treatments and the failures that hope really is never too far away to come find you in your corner, the only person in a room who's a weeping mess. Hope finds you, grabs you, hugs you, and says, *Don't listen to them, just because they said it doesn't make it true. All that's true is Me.*

Hope is coming.

CHAPTER 20

Yes, a Thousand Times, Yes!

$\mathcal{I}$ met my husband when I was seventeen years old. He transferred into my high school the year after I started and the two of us managed to run parallel to one another for over a year and a half. I didn't exactly think highly of him, mainly because there was a lot of hype around this guy, and I wasn't one for following the trend. But man, fall semester of our senior year, he walked into my government class with a fresh tan, bulked football muscles, and the Southern boy mop hair. He plopped down in the seat right in front of me and I am not going to pretend I didn't drool over those muscles instead of learning the basics of our branches of government.

I am here to tell you, I won't pretend for a single second that our love story is straight out of a Nicholas Sparks novel. That being said, the reality is that there is something spectacular about him but even more so, there is something phenomenal about us.

When we were together, the world around us was just a blur. Things didn't feel so plagued with drama and hardship, a failed economy, and hard moments; things felt like healing and fun, friendship and laughter. I felt like I had found the best friend I had been looking for all my life. He was easy to talk to and he listened to everything with intention. I never had to wonder where his attention was. That alone was a gift I didn't realize I had never opened before in my life.

Just a few weeks before we became an official couple, on a February day in 2010, it snowed in our town. We were living in the deep south of Alabama where snow makes an appearance every eight to ten years. It's a marvel: the town shuts down, we all play outside in rubber boots and our sad excuse for winter coats, and then spend the rest of the day eating heavy soups and bread and watching old movies.

My plans consisted of staying home, studying for the ACT, and then binge-watching the Netflix DVDs my mom had ordered for us. (*Lost* Season 3, to be exact.) That is, until my sister invited me to go with her on a drive around the city to see the snow on all the buildings, our church in particular.

Driving in the snow isn't exactly wise in the South. We don't have the machines and infrastructure for it so basically my sister was asking me to go drive on black ice and because I was eighteen and stupid, I said yes.

Both of my sisters ended up hopping in the car; they drove me all around town. We even went to a gas station and bought snacks for the occasion. I mean, why not grab a Dr. Pepper and gummy worms for the thrill of the decade? We started driving back toward the house, and were coming around a big curve on our street when I saw someone standing on the sidewalk in front of our yard. My sisters pulled into the driveway and put the car in park. They turned to me with giddy faces. "That's Cody Bell; he's asking you to prom." Instant panic hit as I realized I hadn't brushed my teeth that day and I was still wearing my pjs. But I got out and he turned to face me.

"Hey!" I said. "What're you doing here?"

"Come out into the road with me!" he said, reaching his hand out toward me to pull me into the street with him.

I obliged.

"Read your yard," he said in a calm, tender voice. I turned to my front yard, where he had written out in the snow, "Will you go to Junior-Senior with me?" (Junior-Senior is what conservative Christian schools call prom.)

I turned and smiled. "YES! A thousand times, YES!" I smiled back at him, jumping up and down. I was honestly shocked he asked, and giddy and nervous. But like any other time when Cody was around, the world around me seemed to just disappear. As we were walking back up my driveway toward the house, I stopped and looked around.

"Hey, where's your car?" I asked.

"Oh, my mom wouldn't let me drive in the snow," he said.

"So how did you get here?"

"I walked." He smiled.

"That's over five miles!" I was shocked!

"I know; I was bundled," he said as he winked at me.

Prom was everything we dreamed it would be, and more. A night of a fancy dinner followed by a dance party that, to this day, is the most fun I have ever had. We danced and sang and had the time of our lives. Life that year was hard. The kind where you sort of freeze and shut off certain parts of your brain so you don't have to think about the sad parts, the parts that are completely out of your control. And that prom was a night that let me remember that life can be full of a lot of nasty surprises that grip you and don't let go until it's all over. But there are also the good surprises, the healing ones that pick you up off the ground and make you better, the ones that make you smile. My Cody was one of those surprises. He showed up, slid into my texts, walked five miles and asked me to prom where he knew every song, and wasn't afraid to dance his heart out with me in front of all of our friends.

The two of us would end up, through a lot of other obstacles, going to college together. A small private Christian college with rules that seemed to be a mile long. But we loved it. We made the best friends of our lives there; we fell deeper in love and grew stronger in our faith.

But most nights, we were bored. Unlike the rest of our pals who went on to state schools with freedom and all types of things to do, we spent most nights going on walks, stargazing, eating late-night Taco Bell, and playing intramural sports with our social clubs (aka sororities for Christian colleges).

One particular fall night, Cody and I decided to go stargazing. This was our thing, our time where we would go talk and reflect and unpack life together, just us and the stars and every thought we have ever had. It was the fall—gorgeous weather and the stars were perfect. Cody met me outside my dorm around midnight and the two of us walked to the school football field to stargaze. Just as we had slid through the iron gate to the field, we heard a car coming down the gravel drive that led to the field. We immediately dropped to the ground and laid flat on our backs. It was security. A bunch of power-hungry students with badges, looking to get other students in trouble.

Cody looked at me. "When they get behind the field house I want you to sprint to the fence, hop over it, and hide under the bleachers." I looked at him like he was crazy. I am 5'11" and spent the entirety of my life dancing. There is no level of sprint within a single inch of my body.

I looked at him. Like he was crazy. "Are you nuts? I can't sprint and I absolutely cannot hop a fence."

"You have to. You can't just stay here!"

"Yeah, I can. You save yourself and I will just take one for the team. They won't suspect anything if it's just me."

"Laura, you can do it; just run," he said to me, hopping the fence. I was barely to my feet. I got up and started running as fast as I could. Cody was standing on the other side of the fence waiting for me to get to him, his arms outstretched toward me. I started putting my feet into the links on the chain-linked fence when Cody grabbed me and the back of my Nike shorts and hoisted me over. My legs were bloodied from the fence and half of my rear was hanging out from the wedgie he had just given me.

The two of us slipped under the bleachers to hide as the car made its way back around the football field, this time shining its spotlight over the field, checking it for any trespassers. We laughed and to this day still remember the sheer rush that came over us, running from security.

One day, I was preparing a speech for a Bible study I was going to teach when this story came up and Cody asked me, "What would've happened had you not run?" I laughed. I would've probably wound up with a trip to see the dean the next morning. But the question sparked a deeper question with me: what would've happened had I not run . . . in so many circumstances. There in the middle of that football field, I was sitting with someone who believed in me, was there for me, was going to make sure I made it to where I needed to go when I couldn't believe enough in myself to do it. Thank God I listened. Thank God I got up and ran. Running toward that fence that night remains in my memory; it's a core one I'll never forget.

Sometimes I feel like there is a timer ticking and waiting for us to get caught in freeze mode because we are too scared to move forward, too scared of what someone might think, too scared to say out loud that something really did hurt us, too scared to. . . . fill in the blank. Every single disappointment and unmet expectation, every broken promise or the betrayal of friends, take them to Him. Make them the kindling for a new day. Make them feed the fire that's being lit at your feet to run with perseverance the race marked before you.

Every time I run into situations and circumstances that seem way too hard or way too out of reach for me, maybe circumstances where I don't really feel like I am qualified, I picture myself running on that football field with tears streaming down my face, climbing the links of that chain-link fence, and I remember that Jesus is on the other side, waiting for me. He is my validation and He doesn't have an expiration date.

God is waiting on the other side of that fence, arms stretched out, ready to pull you, bloodied and scarred, to the other side so He can exchange your robe of grief and shame for a garment of praise. It's time to pull out that wedgie, put a Band-Aid on those wounds, and dance on the graves of every disappointment, failure, loss, embarrassment, or simply fear of the what ifs, and say, "No more; healing is indeed mine."

I didn't have to work for it; I just got to ride around town, eat gummy worms, and show up back home to an invitation to heal. That is where it all began. All I had to do was say yes, a thousand times yes.

And so do you.

CHAPTER 21

Peachy Desserts

The Church hurt me. The kind of hurt I wasn't sure I could recover from. I stepped into college thinking the Church would equip me, and I was left wounded and reckoning in my head how I would recover, what direction I would go, and how many opinions I would get along the way. Opinions were what scared me the most. I knew in my soul I was done dealing with church people. They were the worst. They used my greatest weaknesses and told me what was wrong with me. They took the things I laid out in confidence and dragged them before the public. I discovered I wasn't unbreakable and I wanted to quit.

I had been married a mere month, fresh out of college with no job and a hundred applications in front of people I would never hear from. Cody was working a job that paid him pennies and worked him like a mule. The two of us were living in a trailer in a small town called Fitzpatrick, Alabama, just south of

Montgomery—a double-wide on a big piece of land. In my time stuck at home, I would clean the house and mow the grass. And I would sit. I would sit in my loneliness and my questions. I hated that there were people out there who didn't like me. I hated that there were people out there who didn't believe me. I hated that there were people out there who misunderstood me. It was the post-college loneliness and a misery beyond words.

I came in one morning from cutting grass and checked my phone. There was a text that read, "Hi, it's Nalin. I want to come over to your house. I'll bring a peach dessert." Before I knew it, I was slapping together a chicken casserole and planning a supper with a friend, her boyfriend, and two of their friends. It was strange. Mainly because these people weren't exactly our friends. We had been acquaintances in college. We ran with similar people, but our lives didn't overflow into one another's lives. We were opposite in every way and here I was, anxious about her coming to my house and wondering why in the world she wanted to be friends with me.

But she came and she brought a peachy dessert, and it was divine. Her boyfriend talked to us about mission work he was planning to do. They went out and looked at the pond in our back yard, and I laughed; for the first time in many weeks, I laughed. Months would go by and the two of us would start planning to see one another more and more. Nalin and her boyfriend came to see us when we moved to a small apartment in the city. In fact, they would come every single Wednesday night at 9:00 p.m. for coffee. We would talk and laugh and unpack our thoughts on life and Jesus and people and every moment of it became more and more healing than I considered possible.

I didn't know that friendship could evolve over peachy desserts. I didn't know that it could heal brokenness either. But it does. That's the thing about peachy desserts. They are sweet enough to make an entry and nourishing enough to last awhile.

I have always wondered about Nalin and why she invited herself over that night. Why did she want to come? Why did she care? We weren't the kind of friends who made desserts and invited ourselves over. Not then. But because of her boldness and peachy dessert, I could show up to her house unannounced, kick off my shoes, sit at her table, and talk my head off while we sipped tea, because coffee is too heavy for us these days.

I wonder sometimes what it means to be seen by the Holy Spirit, and I think sometimes it means a peachy dessert from a friend. When Nalin came over, the Holy Spirit wasn't looking at my loneliness; no, He was looking at my fleeing spirit. The one that was nearly ready to pack my bags and run for the hills. Running from the Church seemed fitting for me. But He knew the moment I left the Church I would soon consider leaving Him too. I don't know if I would have. But that season of life in the trailer wrecked me in ways I didn't know was recoverable. So, the Lord didn't send a friend to help me feel less lonely; He sent the Church to show me who He was. I didn't know where to go and the Lord used a friend and a self-invitation to help me "trust fall" back into the grip of Jesus.

I call that version—the one where we "trust fall" into nudges or we get pushed off the edge by someone else who sees it—"obedience." In that season, I was the one who had to be pushed. Obligation, making face, and being approved of was all I had left to hold on to. And even that was slipping through my fingers.

As Christians, we all know we have to *love* one another, or at least that is what's asked of us. But the reality is, most of us are desperately striving to be *liked.* There will be some—there might even be a lot of—people who don't like you or what you bring with you. There will be tremendous amounts of people who misunderstand you. Here's a friendly, Christ-centered reminder: Jesus was gravely misunderstood and it never took His identity. Don't let someone's opinions or misunderstandings rob your identity when it's right there inside of you, waiting to be used by the One who created you.

It would take me years to undo that. The undoing of others' opinions of me and their hopes for my life. There would be people for years to come who would be so disappointed in my choices, but I had to learn to not lose my heart in the middle of it. I believe wholeheartedly that although the Church can wound people, *because* it's full of wounded people, it can also heal a lot of people…because it's full of healed people.

I spent coffees at 9:00 p.m. learning that I could sit comfortably in conversations with people I didn't agree with theologically and still believe they loved God just as much as me. That year was a reckoning on all of us and made us believe it couldn't be that way. But somehow the Lord sustained me and pushed me forward. He pushed a friendship forward. One that was unlikely and different. One that really didn't make sense. The two of us would laugh when people would ask how we became friends, and we would tell them it was because she invited herself over and never stopped coming. But that's what it was; it was an invitation and a never giving up. Kind of like the Father's heart, inviting us to better things and never letting go.

When Cody started working full time at the family farm, we were still living in Montgomery. He would travel five days a week and I would stay home with Emmy Lou, three hours away, five days a week. We did this for eighteen months. The first months were hard, but as time progressed it got better, we got more used to the distance, and I came up with my own routines and ways of dealing with being away from him. Thursdays at Nalin's was one of them.

By this time, she and her boyfriend had married and they had a baby girl. I'd go to her house for mid-day nap time, and she and I would eat snacks and keep each other company while our girls napped. She was probably the person who saw the raw, the real, and the challenge of me being alone so frequently.

The reality was that Cody and I were exhausted, and our marriage, we feared, would start to take a heavier hit if we were to keep up the distance. We prayed and we considered every option under the sun. We concluded together that moving away from everything we knew was the best decision for our family. I immediately felt it—the fear of how it would hurt others, how they may not understand why, how rejection could all be a part of this decision. We were planted, planted in Montgomery. But God had a different plan.

I spent days, weeks, and many hours praying and wondering how I would tell anyone, especially all my closest people, that we were leaving. I grieved it before I spoke it out loud. I even, like Jonah, tried to weasel my way out of it a couple of times.

One night, I went to Nalin's house to hang out. I had a babysitter and an evening to myself and spent it hanging out with her and her little family. Her husband left the room briefly to get something for us and Nalin got a really serious look on her face. She reached her hand across the couch to me and grabbed my hand.

"Lars. I want you to know. If you need to move, if you need leave, it's okay to go." Out of nowhere. Unprovoked. Having no idea that in just a week Cody and I would be telling her and her husband, our very best friends, that we were moving three hours away. I nodded to her and felt like I was going to burst into tears with relief. I never needed her permission. None of us need permission but often, without knowing, we grasp for it. We want to know that what lies ahead is safe. That the telling of the big secret won't lead to a dramatic ending but in love and good measure. Often, the carrying of the secret is harder than the releasing.

I felt like I was going to burst. But it was from the fear of man. It was from the fear that I couldn't do what I set out to do because of what others might think. It's okay for someone to be wrong about you. It's okay for them to misunderstand your choices and your hopes and fears and dreams. Around the corner is always someone who still says yes to your hopes and brings peachy desserts, or holds your hand and says, "It's okay. Choose the life the Lord has for you. Don't give up; it's only going to get better."

A few months after we moved, I was struggling and would text Nalin once a week to tell her how much I missed her. I went to the mailbox one afternoon and had a package from her, a book titled *Will the Circle Be Unbroken: A Memoir of Learning that Everything Is Going to Be Okay*. It was a book I had wanted a for a long time. I sent her a teary video thanking her.

The night of the peachy dessert, the night she told me to go, and the day I received a book in the mail telling me everything was going to be okay are all reminders that the Church still has really strong legs to stand on. They're sturdy and kind and humble and they help heal the broken. More than anything, the Church, when led by the Spirit of God, is a peachy dessert.

Peachy Dessert Recipe

WHAT YOU'LL NEED:

- 1 pkg dry cake mix—white, yellow, or French vanilla
- 1/3 cup butter, room temperature
- 2 large eggs, divided
- 29-ounce can peach slices, drained
- 12-ounce cream cheese, room temperature
- 1/4 cup sugar
- 1 tsp pure vanilla extract

HOW TO PREPARE:

1. Preheat oven to 350 degrees.
2. Spray a 9" x 13" pan with non-stick cooking spray.
3. In a large bowl, mix cake mix, butter, and 1 egg with a fork until you get a crumbly mixture. (Set aside 1 1/2 cups of crumbs for topping.)

4. Press the remaining crumbs on bottom of prepared pan; bake 8 minutes.
5. Dice drained peaches and spread over top of crust.
6. In the bowl of an electric mixer on medium-high speed, beat the cream cheese, sugar, remaining egg, and vanilla extract. Spread over top of peaches.
7. Sprinkle with reserved crumbs. Bake 30 minutes.
8. Chill at least 30 minutes before serving.

Serves 12. Store leftovers in the refrigerator.

CHAPTER 22

Crying in Church

hurch hopping is the worst. It's like dating churches. What does this one have that the other doesn't? Oh, Lord in Heaven, have You church hopped lately? It might be sacrilegious to say, but I think church hopping is from the devil himself. You're always new and showing up in hopes that someone notices that you're the lost puppy in need of a good home. But also, please don't put a leash on me; I'm not ready. For two years we were in a church struggle, starting and changing and starting and changing and starting and changing again, all while still being new at every single dang thing. While being new has its advantages, especially in a small town, I found myself crying every Sunday. (Ever heard of the Sunday scaries?)

Cody and I trudged through a wilderness of sorts as we left behind friends, family, and a church that knew my great, great grandmother, and learned how to be new again. We learned most days that, just when we thought we understood how this little town works, we find out it's Thursday and apparently the whole town closes on Thursdays.

And church. People stare, ask the same questions, friendly and unfriendly. You know the regulars, the people who clearly know everyone and volunteer for everything under the sun. You know the regulars that don't want new people. (How's that one for a church reputation?) And yes, I have repented for every new family that darkened the doors of my home church to whom I never introduced myself. Because now I am new and my future, right now, seems to be here in this small town that has a pace of its very own. I realize I need people to see me and talk to me and show me how to get to the nursery and where the bathroom is and maybe even invite me to lunch.

So, at first, I cried every Sunday.

If anyone tries to tell you that leaving your hometown or your home church or traditions you once loved or a community of friends you spent years cultivating or a community of faith is an easy thing to do, they're lying. Straight through their teeth. The greatest fib ever told. Don't let Instagram fool you. It has felt like daggers, like a surgery of sorts. Somedays, it still does.

It felt so good to quit hopping around and finally settle down in a church. One that kept popping back up to us as the "best for us as a whole family" and where we could finally start to dig our heels in. People are starting to know us. Sometimes I have wondered if they have some special welcoming committee with earpieces telling them who is new because of how well this church welcomes newbies. They say hello and include us and invite us, and now, this place is starting to feel like home. And yes, the first Sunday that we circled back to this congregation (the first one we ever visited), I held back tears the whole service. Not because I was unhappy, but the anxious emotion was stronger than anything else around me.

Yes, I cried that Sunday.

A few weeks ago, I asked for prayers in Sunday school. I was feeling nervous about an upcoming doctor's appointment that was a plane ride away. I didn't tell anyone about the appointment, just the trip. I was consumed with stress. Every corner of my life had gone through massive transition and I realized about a year too late that it was the greatest source of stress for me. My physical health was beginning to decline because of it and I didn't want people to know. After all, we were still new. I didn't want to become the topic of closed conversations.

After class, a girl approached me. "Tell me about your trip to St. Pete." I smiled and shared that it was for a doctor's appointment. I had to figure out what was causing some health issues as of late and apparently the doctor I was planning to see was best in the biz. I barely shared that I had experienced a response to stress and wanted to get it checked.

Within what felt like thirty seconds, this girl shared a small glimpse into her own story and something unraveled inside me. Like a curtain pulled back on what I had been trying so hard to not let go of. Remember what it was like in college when you felt all consumed and you called your mom? She said nothing but, "Hello?" and just the sound of her voice gave you permission to release a tsunami of tears. That girl at church was the voice that gave way to release for me. We talked about life and stress and the Enneagram and books we loved and thoughts and Jesus— and I felt the Lord come straight into the room. We skipped the whole church service, sermon and all, and I realized that nothing was more ministerial than sitting and doing church in the way that Jesus would have: stopping for the one who couldn't carry it all anymore.

This girl. She was the same girl who had invited me to choir practice my first Sunday visiting, not having a clue if I could carry a tune. But a potluck lunch was involved, so obviously it was a yes. She even drove me home after. But this day, she took a moment and hugged me and saw the level of stress I had carried for nearly two years and said, "Bring on the rain."

That Sunday I cried in church.

Because for the first time in a long time, church felt like home again. I've come full circle. I'm a year in to being a part of this family, more importantly a year into a friendship with the one girl who stopped to love on me the way I so desperately wanted to be loved on.

I used to believe that I would live in my hometown forever. My roots would be dug down so deep nothing in all the earth could dig them up. I believed that everything in my life would be seen from that perspective. That was the one dot on the map that made sense to me even if the town wasn't all that great. I thought my parents would stay too and my siblings and their families. But one by one we have been plucked out—by jobs, by marriage, and I think for me, straight force.

I believed in where I lived for so many years, so much so it became my identity. I didn't even realize that until it came time for me to tell all my people that we were leaving. And I realized I had made a location a place of identity instead of a place of ministry. I never knew that a soul could do such a thing but there is a real power sometimes in feeling like the one who knows it all and being the one people turn to for help.

I have rummaged through our old things. Yearbooks and t-shirts and memories of a place that I know my kids won't know or experience the way I did. And that's okay. But for a while there, it wasn't. I couldn't let it go. Saying yes to a new place God had for me felt like I was losing myself, not relocating.

Moving to this tinier dot on the map taught me that I can live in so many different places and it will never dictate who I am. (Well, it can, but only if I let it.) The identity piece feels tricky, a ground we never want to walk upon because it's messy. It brings up bad patterns and old wounds. But it also stirs up the idols and the images we all like to carry around in our back pockets and hope our shirt tail can cover it up.

My in-laws move every eighteen months. No lie. It's insanity. And not only do they move, but they move cities and cross state lines. Cody went to fourteen different schools before the eleventh grade. Since we started dating, my in-laws have moved seven times. In those seven times they have changed states and cities. Only one of those moves was in the same town, from a rental to ownership. I used to look at them like they were crazy. Sometimes I still do.

For years I believed that it was only right, only good and quality parenting, to stay in one place, live near family, etc. It seemed foolish to me in many circles to watch people who willingly moved far away for no good reason. *Why wouldn't you stay? Build the life that you had? Dig down your roots?* But now, I am the one who has moved cities. I became the new person. I left my roots. I found new ones. I made memories with my family that would've never have been made had we stayed. The adventure was daunting, but it was bonding. It brought me new friends, new ideas, space for learning, and a chance to grow and expand. It gave me a sense of understanding of who I am. And no place makes up who we are; it's who we are that makes up a place.

That's why new friends at century-old churches in town can become the best friends you could ever hope to link arms with. It's why we cry at church, because we realize that crying gets rid of all the weight we have been carrying around and gives us space to be us again.

CHAPTER 23

Finally Home

The last three years have been a series of undoing and finding a new way of living. I had to learn how to unhook my high heels that I let sink down into the thick, wet, prairie soil of south Alabama and put on some boots to move a few hours north. People may roll their eyes when they hear some-one "complain" or even grieve moving from the city to a small town that bears a striking resemblance to Stars Hollow. They may even laugh when I say how sad I have felt living on nearly one thousand acres of land I never spent a dollar acquiring.

But here's the deal: I am all about feeling like I belong. I'm a deeply connected and loyal friend who would prefer living my life surrounded by a dusty, old box of old friends, family, stories of my ancestors, and the sound of my dad singing "The Old Rugged Cross" with his booming bass voice. I love the con-nection that comes with family and noise and memories and sto-ries. I have lived most of my life making decisions only after I have run them by the closest thirty people in my life, a personal board of directors if you will. Deep down, every time I watch an episode of *Everybody Loves Raymond*, I wish I was Italian so I could feel the deep, rooted, personal connection of an authentic Italian family. I want the loud, the fights, the food, and the touch. I wish it didn't feel unnatural to me to kiss every person I see on the cheek, for good measure. Maybe in Heaven I'll be a natural kisser so people can feel my warmth every time they hug me.

Leaving home and leaving my home church nearly broke me. No more inside jokes and best friends to pop over and see. No more food from my favorite local restaurant, where people knew me by name and hugged me when they saw me around town. My cousins and aunts and uncles whom I saw weekly at church would now be my Christmas family, and I couldn't bear the thought of stepping into a church that didn't know who my parents were, let alone my grandparents and great-grandparents. The depth to which this rocked me was so sickening I could hardly take it.

Within the first few weeks of moving away, I received a call that our previous next-door neighbor had passed away. She had lived a long, good life but it was still sad. The two of us had become comrades of a sort. Some days I would walk next door and sit on the brick wall in her back yard while she shared her stories of fleeing Hitler and the detention camps her family escaped, the arranged marriage turned magical love story, and all her favorite things about her grandkids. She was a soul sister, even though we were sixty years apart in age. I called Cody on my way home to tell him that we were going to Montgomery for the weekend and to be ready to leave the next day.

We spent the weekend in Montgomery doing all our favorite things. We attended the funeral, hugged her kids and grandkids, and stayed long enough to go to our home church for a service before heading back to the farm. At church, we sat through the service, which felt off and strange and not the same since Covid. Afterward, I stood in the lobby and hugged every neck that could find me. I was desperate to feel known again in a place of familiarity. I smiled and hugged dozens of people who have known my family for years.

Two ladies approached me, two who have known me like the rest, but maybe a bit deeper. Mrs. Cindy and Mrs. Jodi, sisters-in-law. Blonde, Barbie-doll women. Both mothers to kids I grew up with. Cindy's sons were my age and some of my best friends in high school and Mrs. Cindy was always my favorite chaperone on church trips. A second mom of sorts. Mrs. Jodi is a natural kisser, someone who hugs and gives you a kiss on the cheek just because she's saying hey. She was the first person in my life who made me believe that being almost six feet tall was actually a decent thing. Once, in the bathroom of church, she looked me over with a big smile on her face. I was sixteen and painfully slumped over, trying to not be the Jolly Green Giant in every room. Jodi's eyes glistened as she smiled and smacked on a piece of gum, "Wanna know what's great about being us? We tall girls are optical illusions. Out of all your friends, everyone in the group could gain twenty pounds and you would be the only one nobody would notice it on. Stand up straight." I've never stood taller than in that moment.

The two of them found me that fall morning in 2020, in my most emotional and fragile moment. Cindy hugged me; Jodi too.

The two of them stood there and looked at me; Cindy grabbed my hands and with sincerity unlike anything I have ever felt before she said, "How is the farm . . . really?"

I looked at her, trying to muster up some sort of pretty answer that didn't sound like I was faking it, but in that moment all I could do was crumble into a puddle of tears that had been stirring around in my gut for roughly two months. I crumbled, knowing that someone who knew me and had known me the way I so desperately love being known could see straight into my eyes and know that I was so sad.

"I'm so lonely, I'm so lonely, I'm so lonely . . . " I kept saying in between sobs. I couldn't get anything else out except that. The two of them stood there and held me while I released the built-up tension of uprooting my life and attempting to live it somewhere else. Being known, man. There really is nothing quite like it.

It's been almost three years since that conversation.

Someone asked a question in church last night, "What is something that the Lord asked you to do that was the harder choice but the better one?" I turned to a friend and quickly said, "Moving here."

She looked back at me and said, "If you never moved here you would've never met me." The two of us have become good friends since finding this church and my heart felt known for a moment and deeply proud. Proud that I had begun the journey of laying the roots that I so desperately missed. One step, one new friend, one new church, one new grocery store path at a time.

What I have learned is that I can stand, even without traditions and roots, without the solid foundation of being known.

I can go on even when my sense of belonging that I relied so heavily on is completely gone. It's like slamming your pinky toe into a wall corner too quickly and trying to walk it off, and wailing as you move through the pain. One step, another, three more until all of the sudden, the pain is gone, and you start to feel like you again. Call it resilience, call it acceptance; maybe it's a little bit of both. But I know what it's like to leave a piece of yourself behind to follow the path you know the Lord put you on, even if it wasn't the easier choice.

I returned back home to Montgomery for the Easter Sunday Service in 2022. I knew I would get to see everyone because it was Easter, so all the natural non-churchgoers would appear out of the woods to pay their one-Sunday-a-year respects. I walked over to the fellowship hall of the church to bring Emmy Lou to the children's activities. As I entered the doors, I immediately saw Jodi. She and I made eye contact and she beelined in my direction. She smiled and said, "Laura Jean, it sure does feel good to see you." As she hugged my neck and kissed me on the cheek, I returned the mutual joy and affection I had for her. She grabbed my hands. "Let's try this again," she said. "How is the farm, really?" I smiled at her. She nodded, "Sounds better already."

Something strange happens when we go home. We manage to find out that we are braver than we think, stronger than we imagined, and even more loved than we dreamed of being. I have a hard time moving forward unless I know what's coming next. But when it comes to going home, I don't have to wonder. I just get to sink back into it. Coming home is refreshing, it's healing, it's renewing. I get to just simply be. I don't have to try to plan for things that simply don't make sense. Coming home helps me say yes to tomorrow. It helps me see all the years I lived out the unknowns that scared me so crapless and survived, and guess what, I was still loved and seen and chosen and wanted.

When the prodigal son ran home, he didn't expect to be upheld and honored and thrown a party; he just wanted his Father. He just wanted to go home and hear someone say, "I know you. No matter how hard it is, I know you and I love you. No matter where you went and how bad you messed up, I am going to stand in the gap for you and wait until the day you come home and smile because you made it through another hard thing."

I wanted to give up when I planted myself in Arab. That new place felt raw and nothing like the cozy pair of socks I envisioned. But, I kept going. More and more I realize that one day, I am going to be the church youth trip chaperone. Kids will talk to me and think of me as a second mama and show up back home after a big life change. I hope to God I get to stand in their gaps and let the floodgates rush out while they process newness and hardships and hormone-induced cry sessions. Because one day I'll be someone else's home; I just have to build mine first. And the more I realize I always have a home in God, the easier that is to do here on Earth.

Home is my people. It's safety and security. It's inclusion and connection. It's healing and hope and reconciliation. It's Jesus.

Some of us have homes that aren't filled with the good people or the church lady whose purse smells like Juicy Fruit gum. Some of us are stuck with tragedy and heartache and a nightmarish hell no person should go through.

But home is still yours to make. To redo. To run to. To grab the hem of the garment and give the last penny you have to. Because home is the presence of Jesus. Home is Jesus. And He is here. All for the taking. When this life is over and the smells and moments and people and anxiety and sickness and fun and grief are all gone, it is before HIM that you will stand and it's the greatest place you could ever be. Home. You can always come home.

About the Author

*L*aura Bell is a writer, speaker, podcast host, and storyteller who was born and raised in the Deep South of Montgomery, Alabama. She is a wife to her high school sweetheart, Cody, and the mother to two children, Emmy Lou, Oaks, and Lottie

Laura is known for finding joy among the sharp edges of life and adding a little Southern spice to it. She graduated from Faulkner University with a Bachelor's degree in English Literature, which pushed her to start a blog upon graduation focusing on finding hope, buried deep in the nooks and crannies of the Deep South. Laura had the honor of endorsing Sean Deitrich's (also known as "Sean of the South") latest book, *You Are My Sunshine*.

Today, Laura resides with her husband and children on their family farm in the small community of New Harmony, Alabama.

www.laurabell.co

A free ebook edition is available with the purchase of this book.

To claim your free ebook edition:

1. Visit MorganJamesBOGO.com
2. Sign your name CLEARLY in the space
3. Complete the form and submit a photo of the entire copyright page
4. You or your friend can download the ebook to your preferred device

Morgan James
BOGO™

A **FREE** ebook edition is available for you
or a friend with the purchase of this print book.

CLEARLY SIGN YOUR NAME ABOVE

Instructions to claim your free ebook edition:
1. Visit MorganJamesBOGO.com
2. Sign your name CLEARLY in the space above
3. Complete the form and submit a photo
   of this entire page
4. You or your friend can download the ebook
   to your preferred device

Print & Digital Together Forever.

Snap a photo

Free ebook

Read anywhere